MW01118340

THE NEW MOM SELF-CARE MASTER PLAN

DISCOVER THE POWER OF TAKING CARE OF YOURSELF, AVOID THE CONSTANT BURNOUT, AND EXPERIENCE THE JOY OF MOTHERHOOD

OLIVIA ROSE

CONTENTS

INTRODUCTION

When pregnant, you've probably heard so many clichés and wonderful words of wisdom, such as, *"For every baby born, a little sun rises," "There is no greater happiness than seeing your family grow," "A new baby is like the beginning of all things – wonder, hope, a dream of possibilities,"* or *"Being a mom is the greatest experience in the world."*

While these are sweet and inspiring words that are supposed to excite, motivate, give you comfort, and make you believe that your nine months of getting fatter, sicker, emotional, clumsier, and forgetful will be worth it at the end, you just can't resonate with any of them after welcoming your bundle of joy. Reality kicks in!

No doubt, motherhood can be quite exciting and exhausting – it has its ways of flipping life upside down and demanding more than you thought you were incapable of. One minute, you feel like you're on top of every situation and doing amazingly well, and the next, you feel like you don't know who you are. Not only is it a challenge to always keep your babies safe and alive, but it's also hard for you to have your sense of self after birthing a child.

The most surprising part of being a mother was how fragile our mental health can be after giving birth. It's so strange because we've most likely heard stories from other mothers who struggled. Still, for some reason, we don't resonate until we have our fair share of experiences to which we can relate.

For me, when I got pregnant with my first child, my whole mindset shifted from the one of ME to never-ending WE's. The reality of caring for another human was beyond my comprehension, and I finally agreed that there's a lot to know before the arrival of a baby. Even after my second baby, I was consumed with ensuring that the life forms I created were always healthy and happy.

It always felt like I had no control over my life and time. I wanted to be always there for my kids and, at the same time, not lose my identity. I wanted to be that hot girl who was happy, bubbly, and energetic without feeling guilty or blaming myself. I neglected myself and did everything for my family at the expense of my mindset and well-being.

Thankfully, even if it took so long, all that came to a halt one afternoon in the park. I've just had my third baby this time, and her older siblings were still under five years old.

With the latest addition to my family, everything became too much for me to handle. And now, my idea of motherhood was clearly a hazy and dream-like state.

So, while sitting on a bench at the park to ensure the kids get some fresh air, I watched my two older kids run around with giggles, having their best life and obviously happy. My newborn was in her stroller, looking at me with her beautiful blue eyes.

I was surrounded by their positive energy, but I couldn't soak it all in. I just burst out crying. In my head, I was like, *"Olivia! What's wrong with you? Why aren't you happy? Your kids are happy and healthy. But why are you in such a dark place?"*

In that moment of my darkness, my mom's words came through. I always quizzed her on why she always watches Jane Fonda's Workout tape and followed her instructions, wrote in a big book, and said affirmations. She replied: *"You can never pour from an empty cup. That's my own way of filling my cup."*

My dad was always away due to work, and my mom did an amazing job caring for four kids and manning the fort. She was always a positive light to me, and remembering her words awakened something inside me.

After my mini breakdown in the park and some time alone for self-reflection, I knew that I needed to take better care of myself to thrive as a mom. I just had to save myself; I was the only one who could do it for ME. So, I resolved that self-care will be a priority in my life.

So the next day, I got into my workout gear, laced up my shoes, and asked my husband to keep an eye on the kids while I took a run. As I walked to the door, the mom's guilt set in, and I was convincing myself to stay back. But when I thought back to the day before in the park, I said to myself, *"I can't go back!"* And then I set out and had a good run.

The next day, my muscles were tired, and another run wasn't an option. So, I brought out a journal and started writing my thoughts. I've always loved writing but stopped because I felt I didn't have the time. But with every letter I wrote, I felt different feelings welling inside me – bliss, joy, and excitement. Yes, I was onto something! As I walked around the house that day, I had this sense of elation beaming out of me that even my kids and husband noticed. He looked at me and muttered, *"Who is this new woman? I've missed her so much."*

So that experience triggered my journey back to wellness and self-care. And while being a mother is easily one of the hardest things I've ever gone through in my entire life, I am so incredibly grateful for it and the lessons it has taught me, and the passion it has instilled in me.

Like my old self, you've probably neglected yourself. You lack sleep and energy to get through the day without feeling drained and beaten. You always think you aren't doing enough as a mom. You don't sleep well at night; even when the baby sleeps, you're engaged with your overdue to-do lists from the day before. These have made you overwhelmed, lose concentration, make clumsy mistakes, get irritable with loved ones, and argue over the littlest things.

But what if I tell you that practicing self-care can help transform your life and improve your physical and mental well-being? Self-care isn't luxury or being selfish; it is the act of making a deliberate choice to engage in activities that cater to your well-being.

As you read this book, you'll discover that it's okay, even as a new mom, to prioritize your needs and wishes rather than constantly feeling like you're sacrificing yourself for your family. You'll learn how to do this in a compassionate and caring way.

You'll discover that you don't have to change your whole life to engage in self-care. You don't need to go on a week-long Yoga retreat, spend so much on massages, or live a luxurious lifestyle to engage in self-care. Even an act as simple as eating ice cream, flossing, getting a new hairdo, or praying can make a lot of difference – it changes everything. And if you think you don't have enough time for self-care, I will prove to you that you have more than enough through this book.

After overcoming the guilt of putting my needs first, I discovered that even as little as 10 to 15 minutes a day for

'Me' time made a massive difference to my family. Knowing first-hand how difficult motherhood can be and seeing the struggles of many moms, I got inspired to write this book as a way of sharing how I was able to overcome the guilt and shame I felt for many years, and the effective self-care routines that pulled me out of the rot I was in. So other new moms won't have to go through the same struggles.

By sharing my knowledge, I believe other moms will see the importance of overcoming their fears and prioritizing themselves. This book is a collection of my years of experience as a mother of three children and personal research from credible studies.

Being a new mom can be incredibly isolating. However, as you read this book, know someone out there has your back. Remember, you aren't alone. Many moms have walked in your shoes, and after adopting self-care and choosing what it means to them, they're smashing their goals and brimming with happiness.

Among many is singer Pink who feels that self-care is about learning to say no and having boundaries. On the other hand, actress Kerry Washington believes that eating right as part of self-care isn't about fitting into skinny jeans but eating to feel strong.

While motherhood may not be what you have imagined, it's best to look on the bright side and enjoy the ride.

Trust me; it will remain one of your most cherished moments.

I can't wait to see you creating your ideal identity, being who you've always wanted to be, and living life on your terms.

Buckle up, and let's get started!

1

LOVING YOUR POST-BIRTH BODY

"It was like 'oh my god, this is not my body.' It was literally like I had a fat suit on, and I sat staring at the mirror crying."

— KEIGHLY LEWIS

When a baby is born, so is a mother. Being a mother involves a process of transition to motherhood which is often accompanied by many changes. If you notice, you'll see that after birthing, your body is changing, your emotions are screaming aloud, and your hormones are going wild, even though your heart is swirling with your love for your baby.

But what about your insecurities? How do you see yourself after all that has happened to your body? What body image do you have of yourself? Do you look at yourself and feel confident about how you look? Or do you look at yourself and wish you had looked different?

The fact remains that your body image is important to staying healthy – it shapes how you do everything.

Like most women who had just given birth to a baby, I unnecessarily stressed over my postpartum body, especially after my second child. I will look at my body and resented what pregnancy had put my body through two times! I remember standing in front of the mirror one day and unfairly picking apart every change I noticed. I saw raw nipples, hair loss, weird-looking boobs, nipple discharge, stretch marks, acne, swelling in my legs and face, and linea nigra (the dark vertical line on my belly).

The scrutiny continued until after my third baby. I was able to pull myself together and make peace with my new body. Looking back, I can confidently say I've come a long way. I realized there are many ways to love my postpartum body, even if it doesn't look how I envisioned it.

So, to take a deeper look at what is happening on the inside and the outside of a woman's body and how to start accepting our body and the changes happening. This chapter will discuss women's hormones and ways to help the body recover from what it has been through.

It's time to talk about the real truth about postpartum bodies!

THE TRUTH ABOUT YOUR POST-PREGNANCY BODY

A lot happens in your body right after giving birth to your baby. Even before giving birth, your body has worked hard to ensure your baby is safe and healthy. And now that you've given birth, the changes don't stop.

After childbirth, your womb will start to shrink and return to its original size at around six weeks postpartum. This happens to allow all your internal organs to find their places. Remember how heavy you were breathing in your third trimester? Well, it will stop now as your lungs will get more space with the new changes.

Your diastasis recti and separate abdominal muscles will slowly start recovering and finding their way closer to each other. As for your abdominal muscles, the fastest time for their recovery is during the first two months after birth. However, it can slowly heal and might need a year or longer if the separation is large after delivery. So, even though it takes about 6 weeks for the womb to return to its usual shape, it can take up to a year for the abdominal muscles to fully recover.

During childbirth, your vagina and pelvic floor muscles will stretch, making you experience tearing and bruising (in some cases). Thankfully, there's good blood circulation in the vagina, which helps it heal quickly, leaving no scars. You may notice that your vagina swells after childbirth;

this will decrease rapidly over time. The recovery for the vagina should take a few weeks to complete, and the pelvic floor function should return to normal after three months. Overall, full recovery should take one year.

If you have done a C-section, your abdominal wall, uterus, and skin will need time to heal. The initial healing will happen between four to six weeks after birth and continues.

Regarding weight, you would have gained extra pounds during pregnancy, and you expect to start shedding some off immediately after birth. The average weight loss for moms after birth is 13 pounds. And after six weeks, the remaining weight should be adipose tissue which is a body fat or connective tissue that extends throughout your body.

The initial weight loss will start when you give birth to your baby. Your baby, placenta, amniotic sac, and other fluid have left your body, relieving you of some weight. And over the next six weeks, other fluids will start returning to pre-pregnancy levels, and you'll continue to lose weight.

Note that every woman is different when it comes to losing postpartum weight. A 2018 study by McKinely et al. revealed that only 20% of women would regain their pre-pregnancy weight within the first three months after giving birth. 80% of women need more than 3 months to return to their pre-pregnancy weight, and 24% will have at least 10 pounds even one year after postpartum.

So, don't be hard on yourself when you aren't losing weight as expected. Give yourself a break and know everyone's weight loss journey is different. Focus on bonding with your newborn and enjoying every moment.

WHAT'S GOING ON WITH YOUR HORMONES

Having a baby is a beautiful and life-altering moment. It is a point where your body undergoes not only extreme physical changes but also chemical changes.

Your hormones are chemicals that act as messengers in your body. Estrogen and progesterone are the primary reproductive hormones that prepare your body for pregnancy. Other reproductive hormones are secreted by the ovaries.

Your progesterone will increase rapidly during pregnancy to prevent you from delivering your baby prematurely. While estrogen prepares the uterine lining for your baby and maintains the pregnancy.

During pregnancy, the placenta will grow within your uterus to provide nutrition and improve blood supply to the fetus. The uterus secretes hormones to support your pregnancy.

Other reproductive hormones are prolactin and oxytocin. Prolactin is responsible for milk production, while oxytocin helps with the production of contraction during labor. It is also involved in milk production and encourages bonding between a mom and her baby.

So far, you've seen the different changes pregnancy brings. But that's not all – you also experience beautiful hair and skin when pregnant. Some women have even reported that they feel fabulous during pregnancy. This isn't surprising because progesterone and estrogen are hormones that create serotonin and dopamine. These are mood-regulating hormones that elevate the mood.

Immediately after birthing your child, your progesterone and estrogen rapidly decrease, regardless of the type of delivery you've had (vaginal or cesarean). With this hormone decrease and the physical and emotional stress you experience during labor and delivery, it shouldn't be surprising to see new moms in a haze in the next few days. Sometimes, it continues for the first few months – postpartum. The sudden decrease in progesterone and estrogen hormones is likely why many moms experience postpartum depression, sometimes called baby blues.

Postpartum depression has been a prevalent issue, and much attention isn't given to it. The American College of Obstetricians and Gynecologists (ACOG) has strongly advised that one postpartum check-up six weeks after giving birth isn't sufficient – we need to do more.

Postnatal care should be prioritized and be an ongoing process for new moms. Unfortunately, that isn't the case. As a result, many moms struggle to access better care after birthing their children.

Based on my experience caring for three kids, I strongly feel that the lack of adequate postpartum care for new moms and hormonal changes contributes greatly to postpartum depression. As moms, we need to prioritize self-care by supporting and protecting ourselves. We only have ourselves and are in the best position to know what's best for us.

TAKE A BREAK FROM SOCIAL MEDIA AND COMPARISONS

With the advancement of technology, we are forced to navigate the fast and ever-growing world of social media. It's evident that social media's impact on our mental health is far greater than the benefits we'll get.

Every day, you're exposed to perfectly curated images of your friends living their best lives, making it easy for you to fall into the trap of comparing your everyday experiences to theirs. As a result, you'd have feelings of inadequacy and unhappiness. Then you start questioning whether you're measuring up to the standards of those around you.

For example, you check your phone, and the first thing you see is a picture of your best friend spending time with her partner and kids at a park or museum. Or maybe they post a picture of their partner helping with chores around the house while they're seated, making videos, and having fun. You then start to question yourself – *why is my partner not pulling their weight on the domestic front? Why am I being left to suffer?*

Thoughts like these can affect your mental health. But it isn't just your mental health that is at stake here. Studies have suggested that social media can also affect your relationship with others. It was revealed that moms who compared themselves to people on social media are likely to feel they're less supported by their network. They also feel bad about their co-parenting relationship with their partner.

I am guessing you've been guilty of comparing yourself with others on social media. How does that make you feel? Does the comparison make you feel less positive about your parenting skill, or does it make you feel empowered as a parent?

Regardless of your thoughts on this, it's important to know that what you see in the media isn't always accurate or the real representation of everyone's life. Maybe you've not been paying much attention, but people tend to share the best parts of their lives online – we don't get to see the ugly sides. They leave out the struggles and challenges they face, which are all part of every human experience.

Instead of focusing on people's lives, focus on your unique experiences and avoid comparing yourself to others. This way, you can avoid the trap of social media-induced sadness and focus on maintaining healthy relationships with people around you.

To avoid overwhelming sadness, you can do a social media detox. This will allow you to pause your social media platforms to boost your overall mood. Whether it's Instagram, TikTok, Facebook, or Twitter, you would've noticed that endless scrolling through them can make you feel more on edge, crummy than chill, and edgy than informed. This should make you consider a social media detox.

Deliberating taking a break from social media can help clear your head, get better sleep, and dial down on anxiety and depression. While a social media detox may sound like a slog, you'll likely feel better after a few days.

As research is still limited, many studies on social media detox suggest that people will feel better after taking a break. They're reported to have a solid sleep and feel less anxious after a social media detox. In a study involving 68 college students, it was reported that most of the participants had mental health benefits from a social media detox.

As you go on a detox and avoid comparison, remind yourself that you're doing way better than you give yourself credit, especially when those negative self-thoughts are creeping up.

According to a popular saying, "Comparison is the thief of joy." So, hold yourself accountable when you're allowing comparison to steal your joy. Consider the advantages and disadvantages of comparing yourself with others. And if anyone is making you feel inferior or less of yourself in any way, it'll be best to avoid the person.

Sticking to your values and what matters to you the most is better. Remember, nobody's life is perfect. So, consider your strengths as you focus on yourself – including how you've been an awesome mom to your little one. Know that you're doing great!

CHANGING YOUR PERSPECTIVE WITH GRATITUDE

Seriously though, how can just expressing gratitude have a positive impact on my life? I remember asking myself this question, and I laughed over the idea of improving my quality of life with gratitude. I'm guessing you also think the same, especially if this is your first time coming across this topic.

Before discussing how gratitude impacts and improves sleep, mood, and even lower blood pressure, let's talk about the science of gratitude and how it affects our brain and body.

What Science Says

Over the past decade, many studies have suggested that people who consciously express gratitude are likely to show expressions and are less depressed. One of those studies that captured the essence of gratitude to the brain was conducted and published in a journal by the University of California, Berkeley. Their recent study took into consideration the problem most research studies previously conducted – which was using well-functioning people in their gratitude research.

By focusing their research on people who struggle with mental issues, the researchers could tell if gratitude is beneficial to their mental state and how it impacts the mind, and bodies of the participants. The study engaged about 300 adults who were mostly college students and were seeking counseling services for their mental health. The majority of these participants struggled with anxiety and depression prior to their counseling.

The researchers randomly assigned the participants into three groups (a, b, and c) while they all received counseling services. Meanwhile, each group was tasked to write different things. Group A was tasked to write a note of gratitude to an assigned partner. Group B was to write about their deepest regrets and negative experiences, while Group C didn't participate in the activities.

After four weeks of receiving mental health counseling, the researchers found that those who wrote a gratitude note daily showed significant improvement with their mental health status compared to the group who wrote down their negative experiences and those who did nothing while receiving mental health counseling.

This suggests that expressing gratitude can significantly benefit brain activity and improve the body's overall state. Meaning gratitude is beneficial for healthy people and to individuals struggling with mental health-related issues by improving sleep, quality of exercise, and lowering anxiety and depression.

In fact, it appears that practicing gratitude while receiving counseling proves to be more effective. Also, compared to the other groups, the group that kept a gratitude journal or note showed greater willpower, focus, enthusiasm, and energy improvements than the other groups.

Furthermore, a similar study by a team of Chinese researchers sorts to understand the effects and reasons behind the combined effects of gratitude and sound sleep on symptoms of anxiety and depression. They discovered that those with higher levels of gratitude were linked to better sleep and showed lower levels of depression and anxiety.

How does gratitude improve depression?

It significantly alters your life experience by teaching your brain to notice and value the little things in life. Having gratitude can improve your overall health, happiness, and well-being while reducing the negative emotions we don't want to experience, such as anger, anxiety, depression, and frustration or irritation, especially during postpartum.

How does gratitude help with sleep?

Scientifically or not, can gratitude really help you sleep better? Of course, I will answer yes since I have had the experience firsthand.

The Journal of Psychosomatic Research suggests that gratitude improves and allows people to get longer sleep. This could result from having positive thoughts and a mind filled with appreciation, especially before you go to sleep.

Furthermore, gratitude directly impacts the brain regions associated with the neurotransmitter dopamine; we know dopamine makes us feel really good. Also, dopamine is known to incite the body into taking action. An increase in the body's dopamine level will likely allow you to do more than you would usually be able to do.

Gratitude list

It takes practice to reprogram the brain to have a more positive outlook. Here are some friendly gratitude exercises that are ideal for giving your brain the right boost and improving your overall well-being:

- Write and keep a gratitude journal of the things you're grateful for.
- Express your gratitude to a friend or coworker.
- Share what you're grateful for with your loved ones.
- Sincerely thank someone when they've been supportive.
- Write or send thank you notes showing your gratitude.
- Recognize and appreciate the beauty of your surroundings and nature.
- Observe when you find the taste and texture of your food satisfying.
- Appreciate yourself because you deserve it.
- Write the things you are grateful for daily on a note and keep them in your gratitude jar. You can easily refer to it when you feel low.

Your brain and overall life can change if you practice gratitude and positive thinking daily for a period! Higher-order thinking abilities like focus and attention are governed by the same brain region as emotions and behavior. Analyzing information can be greatly enhanced by maintaining a positive outlook and keeping the brain happy by practicing gratitude.

WHY SHOULD SELF-CARE BE A PRACTICE FOR ALL NEW MOMS

We can't deny it; being a mom is hard! It entails working all day with endless tasks and errands while still giving your full attention to your baby. Then it becomes more overwhelming when you manage a career, work, or business. With so much time and attention devoted to caring for your little one and the entire family, it's easy to become exhausted and pay no attention to your needs.

You aren't alone if you've neglected your needs and not paid attention to yourself. So many mothers are also guilty of focusing their attention on meeting their children's needs while forgetting theirs.

As I mentioned earlier, you can't pour from an empty cup. So, if you want to provide the best care possible for your kids, you need to care for yourself first.

I remember when Anna reached out to me for help. She narrated how she felt when she held her newborn in her arms – she was over the moon and was genuinely happy. As a new mom, Anna was excited about her journey but soon realized motherhood wasn't as rosy as she thought.

She experienced sleepless nights, never-ending diaper changes, and constant feedings that exhausted her.

As her exhaustion and tiredness persisted, Anna distanced herself from her newborn. She didn't want to touch her little one she couldn't get enough of a few weeks ago. Realizing that she wasn't enjoying parenting, she became determined to prioritize her well-being so she could provide the best care for her baby.

Anna reached out to me, and we worked together to get her out of that phase. She started taking breaks when she felt like and needed to – a relaxing bath or quick nap sufficed. She joined a community of moms for advice and support. She took up meditation and yoga to reduce her stress. Anna found it easier to manage her many activities and her child's behavior in no time. She became refreshed and became a better mom.

When I asked Anna what the most rewarding experience of her life was, she said, "Being a mom!" Luckily, Anna knew that caring for herself was just as important as being a mom.

With determination and ensuring her well-being is a priority, Anna was able to give the best care possible for her child while also maintaining balance in her life. No doubt, Anna's journey as a new mom was challenging, but she could overcome the obstacle and thrived by using the right mindset and support.

Like Anna, many mothers feel overwhelmed and postpone or avoid the things that give them comfort and relaxation. However, mental health specialists continue to emphasize the importance of self-care for moms' physical, emotional, and mental well-being.

Beyond the basic things needed for survival, every mom needs additional efforts for optimized well-being. Even though making time for yourself may seem selfish or indulgent (which it isn't), it is what you need to function well. Small acts of self-care can go a long way in reducing stress, burnout, exhaustion, anxiety, and even depression that new moms feel.

Your body will likely undergo several changes due to hormonal shifts, and it'll take longer for your hormones and body to get back to normal – the more reason you need to start practicing self-care. Even though some changes will stick around longer, acknowledge them and see them as reminders of the remarkable feat (birthing a human) you've just pulled off.

2

SLEEP, EAT, AND EXERCISE – SERIOUSLY?

> "*The world rattling fear of what could possibly happen to my baby if I ever took my eyes off her for 0.5 seconds. I barely slept.*"
>
> — TANESHA SHAYLENE

Sleep…do you even remember what that is? As a new mom, I'm tempted to ask if you get enough sleep daily. But that would be a pointless question – of course, you aren't getting enough sleep.

A 2019 study reveals new moms lose an average of one hour of sleep nightly in the first three months after childbirth. I bet you're thinking about that lost hour right now.

You were up half the night, tending to your crying baby while your partner snored peacefully through the screams. Now it's morning, and your infant is napping soundly. And you're wondering if you should take advantage of that time to crash on the couch or get a quick workout. This is a pretty common scenario for most new moms.

Sleep, diet, and exercise are at the core of self-care for new mothers. All three have a distinct impact on your physical and mental health. In this chapter, we will look at why you need all three and strategies to help you improve each area of self-care.

THE PERFECT TRIAD FOR SELF-CARE

Sleep, diet, and exercise are three critical components of healthy living. They are associated with life expectancy and overall quality of life. They all directly impact our health and well-being, each connected to the other.

As a new mom, keeping all three in balance is important, especially in the early months after pregnancy. Think of your health as a three-legged stool. If one of those legs is shorter, the stool becomes "out of whack" and imbalanced.

You might think that improving one of these factors would benefit you. But while that may be true, improving all three is the key to unlocking numerous physical and mental health benefits – not just for you but your infant.

Diet, sleep, and exercise have a complex relationship that makes them influence one another in innumerable ways.

When any of these lifestyle factors crumbles, it begins a frustrating cycle. A poor diet can affect your sleep, leading to fatigue, making it hard to exercise regularly. It would be best to learn how these three factors impact one another. That is your first step to understanding which lifestyle behaviors you must improve to better your health and well-being.

Sleep

Sleep allows your body and brain to recuperate every day, meaning it affects nearly all tissues in your body. You need a minimum of eight hours of sleep daily. Yet, statistics show that nearly one-third of Americans get under seven hours of sleep daily. This is even truer for new moms.

Poor sleep leads to sleep deprivation, linked to health conditions such as diabetes, stroke, depression, heart disease, and infertility. It also increases the risk of impaired cognitive functions.

Sleep deprivation increases the production of ghrelin, the hunger hormone. At the same time, it decreases the production of leptin, the hormone that gives you that "I'm full" feeling after a meal. But it doesn't stop at that. Poor sleep also causes a surge in insulin – the hormone regulating blood sugar – production.

Together, these hormones can lead to overeating, thus increasing the risk of obesity. Without regular, quality sleep, it's easy to overeat and resort to unhealthy diets.

Losing quality sleep as a new mother in your first few months can impair self-control and decision-making skills. The effects are similar to alcohol intoxication, affecting your reaction times and accuracy. It can potentially put your infant at risk.

Ensuring you get enough hours of sleep every night will not only improve your focus and productivity but also:

- Improve your immune system
- Regulate blood sugar
- Repair your heart and blood vessels

Sufficient sleep is vital for exercise. Not getting as much sleep as you need can make you less physically active during the day, thus reducing your ability to work out.

Exercise

Like sleep, exercise has immense benefits for nearly every system in your body. It isn't just great for your physical health. It also works wonders for your mental health, reducing stress and anxiety. Plus, exercise is widely recognized as an effective tool for fighting depression.

Working out boosts endorphins and "feel-good" hormones. At the same time, it reduces the production of adrenaline and cortisol, which are stress hormones. If you work out regularly, you're probably familiar with what many call a "runner's high," which improves people's mood after a good workout.

Regular exercise has many long-term benefits, including a reduced risk of disease, reduced anxiety, decreased blood pressure, better weight management, improved cholesterol levels, better weight management, and better sleep. Experts call exercise "meditation in motion" because it distracts from stress and anxiety. It also boosts confidence and productivity.

There is irrefutable evidence obtained through substantial research that regular exercise improves sleep. Running, cardio, and other aerobic exercises have been shown to improve sleep quality.

Any amount of physical activity can improve sleep. It can also decrease your risk of insomnia, restless legs syndrome, and other sleep problems.

Diet

Diet and nutrition are the third components of a healthy lifestyle. They have an impact on all aspects of your health. A lack of proper nutrition can affect your sleep quality and activity level. In contrast, healthy, balanced eating can reduce your risk of obesity, diabetes, stroke, heart disease, and other health conditions.

What you eat and when it can also impact your mental health. Certain foods may reduce the risk of anxiety and depression in new mothers.

However, improving your diet alone doesn't offer as many health benefits as combining healthy eating with regular physical activity. Proper nutrition and exercise can decrease fatigue, improve athletic performance, and boost sleep quality. Healthy eating habits can strengthen your immune system and stabilize your mood.

While trying to manage your time as a new, busy mother, I understand if you feel compelled to prioritize the most important things. Unfortunately, the triad of self-care is so connected that you cannot deem one more important than the others.

I have observed that many new mothers try to prioritize diet and exercise. Still, your best bet is to take all three activities seriously and find ways to balance them all.

Let's find out exactly how you can achieve that balance.

REALISTIC REST AND SLEEP ADVICE FOR NEW MOMS

All new parents know that the struggle to get enough sleep is the bane of their lives. Between the diaper changes, multiple feedings, and the crying sessions in the wee hours of the night, you are familiar with that struggle too.

You know that sleep is precious, especially in this stage of parenting. Yet, you cannot bring yourself to get as much sleep as needed. You probably consider sleep deprivation an inevitable rite of passage for new moms. You are willing to deal with it for your newborn. But it would be best if you didn't have to.

Lack of sleep can be draining and exhausting. And if left unchecked, it can trigger many physical and mental health issues.

Caring for an infant is a lot of work. It can be draining, especially for new mothers still recovering from labor. Adjusting to your new life as a parent can be challenging for both parents, but even more so for the mother.

Even if you have an older infant, they can experience disrupted sleep due to teething, a growth regression, or a spurt. If your baby isn't sleeping well at night, neither can you.

Unfortunately, your reality as a new parent is that you cannot control how often your baby wakes up every night. Still, this doesn't mean you're doomed to unending sleepless nights.

Some parents can return to bed, shut their eyes, and fall asleep immediately after a midnight feed. Sadly, life can't be as easy as that for everyone. Many new moms have postpartum insomnia, making sleep impossible to attain.

As you slog through sleep deprivation in the first few months of parenthood, it's normal to wonder if you hope to get through this difficult period.

Enter the wisdom of sleep consultants, which many mothers have used successfully. Based on the best advice from different experts throughout generations, I have some incredibly helpful tips on how to get enough sleep as a new mother.

These tips are all based on one thing: Establishing good sleep hygiene. It may sound like generic advice, but good sleep hygiene makes a difference in maximizing rest after the newborn's arrival.

Creating a wind-down routine and being consistent with your body time prepares your body and mind for sleep. That can be especially helpful if you go to bed right after the baby.

Engage in relaxing activities throughout the day.

You may not know this, but what you do during the day affects your ability to sleep soundly more than what you do before bedtime. Ensure you take time out at different points throughout the day to do something that grounds and relaxes you.

Whether taking a walk, soaking yourself in a bath, or calling a friend for a long chat, ensure you enjoy it. Making grounding and relaxing activities a part of your day keeps stress hormones in check, thus promoting better sleep.

Create a relaxing sleep environment.

This isn't just for you, your baby, and your partner. If you set up your environment for quality sleep, you'll likely get longer daily stretches. Consider this: Does your bedroom make you feel like falling asleep? If it doesn't, that's not a good sleep environment for you and the infant.

It would be best to keep clutter and unfolded laundry out of the bedroom. White noises, dim lights, and the right temp are some of the things that can help make your bedroom relaxing enough for sleep.

Implement a bedtime routine or ritual.

Time is probably the most precious commodity to new parents, and establishing a new routine may be off-putting to you. But even if it's just a few minutes before your bedtime, creating a relaxing bedtime routine can significantly affect the quality and duration of your sleep every night.

A relaxing bedtime routine or ritual can be an excellent way to unwind after working hard during the day to take care of your infant. An ideal way to start the routine is to have a long bath to soothe your mind and muscles. Having a bath is also great for reducing your body temperature, making you more susceptible to sleep.

You can also try journaling before bed to process your feelings and thoughts. That way, you can avoid being kept up by a racing mind after a midnight feeding session. Other things you can include in your routine include turning your electronics off an hour before bedtime, reading a few pages of a book, and listening to soothing music.

Ask for help (and accept it when offered).

New parents don't get a medal for powering through sleeplessness alone. Whenever necessary, ask for help – or hire one if possible. You can even ask friends and family for assistance.

One thing new moms aren't told enough is that it's okay to ask for help or accept it when offered. Whether it's from a friend, family member, or a sleep coach, you can ask for help and accept it.

Take turns.

Often, the best help is your spouse or partner. Teamwork can make a huge difference in parenting. Parents should take turns feeding the baby at night so both can get some uninterrupted sleep.

Suppose you're a nursing mother. In that case, a good approach would be to go to bed at the same time as your baby every night once you've established a nursing relationship. Then, your partner can wake up to feed the baby pumped breast milk during the first wake-up. That will give you a good chunk of sleep for some of the night.

If you're a single parent, remember to ask for help from friends and family – even for overnights.

What about rest?

The general advice is for moms to sleep when the baby is asleep, but this is easier said than done. Usually, moms feel guilty for not using that time when the baby sleeps to do other productive things, like working out or cleaning the home. So, how do you handle that?

The ideal timeframe for a nap is 20 to 30 minutes. Usually, babies sleep uninterrupted for 1 to 2 hours, giving you enough time to nap and be productive. However, if you can't nap, getting some rest can achieve similar effects.

A rest in this context is what we call 'quiet wakefulness.' It's as easy as sitting in your favorite chair, shutting your eyes, and letting a feeling of calmness envelop you. And yes, doing this can be beneficial – although not in the same way as quality sleep.

Resting with your eyes shut can help your mind and body relax. Like sleep, it makes your heart rate slow down and blood pressure drop. As such, resting can:

- Boost your mood
- Reduce stress
- Increase mental clarity
- Boost alertness
- Improve motivation

These are all good benefits but don't replace proper sleep with rest. No matter what, make sure you get enough sleep daily – even if it means hiring help.

HOW TO EFFECTIVELY FUEL YOUR BODY

After childbirth, the first thing at the front of my mind was losing all the pounds I gained during pregnancy. But I quickly learned that eating foods that can fuel my body and give me the energy to be the best mom possible was even more important.

Healthy eating throughout the day is the best way to maximize your energy as a new mom. Breast milk quality stays the same during nursing regardless of what the mother eats. However, the catch is if your body isn't getting all the vital nutrients from your diet, it will provide them from its stores.

Therefore, you are responsible for getting all the nutrients you and your infant need from your meals. It is beneficial for both parties.

You may not be "eating for two," but you have to replenish your body with vital nutrients. Every meal should be half filled with fruits and vegetables, while the other half should be filled with whole grains like oatmeal, brown rice, or whole-grain bread.

Additionally, you should reduce your intake of processed foods and drinks high in saturated fat, salt, and sugar.

The following nutrients should be a regular part of your diet:

- **Protein:** Beans, eggs, seafood, lean meats, and soy products contain high protein levels, which can help you recover from childbirth. Aim for 5-7 servings of protein-rich food per day.
- **Iron:** You need lots of iron so your body can create new blood cells. This is particularly important for new moms who lose plenty of blood during childbirth. Poultry, red meat, beans, and tofu contain high iron content. Aim for 9-10 mg daily.
- **Calcium:** You need 1000 mg of calcium daily – which you can get from three servings of low-fat dairy products.

Here are more healthy foods that should be regular in your diet.

- Salmon
- Low-fat dairy products – cheese, milk, yogurt.
- Lean beef
- Blueberries
- Legumes
- Brown rice
- Oranges
- Eggs
- Whole-wheat bread

- Leafy greens – broccoli, spinach, Swiss chard, etc.
- Whole-grain cereal
- Oats
- Avocados
- Nuts
- Carrots
- Yams
- Chia seeds
- Hemp seeds
- Flax seeds
- Water

New moms generally need 1800 to 2200 calories daily in the early months of parenthood. As a nursing mom, you'll need 500 more calories. Moms breastfeeding more than one baby would need to work out for 45 minutes or higher each day.

Five Healthy Recipes for New Moms

I often meet new mothers who believe they must follow a special diet. And I always tell them they only need a healthy, balanced diet with various nutritious foods.

Here is a list of five healthy recipes you can try.

1. Fruit and Nut Energy Bars

Ingredients:

- 1 cup dried apricots (chopped)
- 2 cups Medjool dates (chopped and pitted)
- ½ cup pepitas
- ½ cup cashews (roasted)
- 3 tablespoons flax meal
- ½ teaspoon cinnamon
- ⅛ teaspoon salt

How to:

- Mix dried apricots and Medjool dates in your food processor and leave until well mixed.
- Add the roasted cashews, pepitas, flax meal, salt, and cinnamon. Pulse until they form a sticky mixture.
- Get some parchment paper and line it with a baking dish. Then, pour the mixture on it and flatten it. Keep in the refrigerator until firm.
- Cut into squares or bars.
- Serve.

2. Turkey and Bean Burrito

Ingredients:

- 1 tbsp garlic (chopped)
- 2 tbsp canola oil
- 1 cup salmon (chopped)
- 1 cup onion (chopped)
- 1-pound ground turkey
- 1 tbsp chili powder
- 1 can of rinsed black beans
- 1 cup sodium-free chicken stock
- ½ tsp dried oregano
- ¾ cup cheddar cheese (grated)
- ¼ cup fresh cilantro (chopped)
- ¾ cup salsa
- 6 large whole wheat tortillas
- 1 large peeled, halved, and sliced ripe avocado

How to:

- Grease a baking dish and preheat your oven to 425 degrees Fahrenheit.
- Heat the canola oil in a big frying pan. Add the chopped onions and stir until it's golden brown.
- Add chili and garlic powder and stir for a few seconds.
- Turn down the heat to medium; add the turkey and stir until it's no longer pink.

- Pour in the beans, chicken stock, and oregano; increase the heat and leave until there's no more liquid.
- Create six portions from the filling and put each in the tortillas. Add some cheese and sliced avocados.
- Roll, tuck, and put the burritos in the greased baking dish.
- Spoon some salsa over each burrito and sprinkle some cheese over it. Put in the oven until the cheese melts.
- Add the cilantro for garnishing.

3. Vegetable Barley Soup

Ingredients:

- 1 chopped onion
- 1 tbsp sunflower oil
- 1 small trimmed and sliced leek
- 3 small peeled and chopped carrots
- 1 clove crushed garlic
- 1 small peeled and chopped parsnip
- 3 sticks of chopped celery
- 100 grams of rinsed pearl barley
- 100 grams of shredded cabbage or kale
- 1 ¼ liter of vegetable stock, hot
- Serve with bread

How to:

- Put a large frying pan on fire; heat the oil and add the onion, celery, parsnip, leek, carrots, and garlic. Season with pepper and salt.
- Cover with grease-proof paper. Put on medium heat and let it simmer for 15 minutes. Stir once or twice.
- Get rid of the paper and add the barley and vegetable stock. Cover again and leave to boil for about 30 minutes or until the barley is tender.
- Add the kale or cabbage and leave to simmer for 1-2 minutes.
- Serve with bread.

4. Quinoa Pilaf with Pine Nuts and Cauliflower

Ingredients:

- 1 cup rinsed and drained quinoa
- 1 ½ cups cauliflower, roasted and steamed
- 2 cups chicken or vegetable stock
- 2 tbsp green olives, chopped
- 2 tbsp pine nuts, toasted
- 2 minced scallions
- ½ tsp of grated lemon zest
- 2 tsp of lemon juice
- 4 tsp of extra virgin olive oil
- Fresh parsley, chopped

- Ground black pepper
- Coarse sea salt

Ingredients:

- Get a small-sized saucepan. Simmer the chicken stock for a few minutes and add the quinoa. Cover for 20-25 minutes until the grains expand.
- Combine the quinoa with all other ingredients. Season with lemon juice, salt, and pepper.
- Serve at room temperature.

5. Cookies

Ingredients:

- 1 cup self-raising flour
- ½ cup butter
- 1 egg
- 1 tbsp flaxseed meal
- 2-3 tbsp of water
- ¾ cup brown sugar
- 1 tbsp vanilla extract
- 2 tbsp brewer's yeast
- ½ cups steel-cut oats
- ½ tsp Himalayan salt

How to:

- Mix the butter and sugar thoroughly in a large bowl. Then, add the egg and vanilla extract and mix once again.
- Add the flaxseed meal and water to a different bowl. Leave for a few minutes.
- Now, add the oats and flaxseed with water to the mixture. Then, make the cookies.
- Put the biscuits on a lined baking tray; flatten them with a spoon. Let it bake for 10-12 minutes.

These cookies are great for stimulating milk production.

Remember that you can make these recipes in large batches and refrigerate them for another day.

YOUR RECOVERING BODY CAN BENEFIT FROM LIGHT EXERCISE

Following a regular exercise routine soon after childbirth can reduce the risk of postpartum depression and improve overall health. The good news is, shedding the extra pounds after giving birth is easier than many think. Remember that new moms don't have the same experience, so you might want to check with your doctor before starting any workout routine.

With that in mind, here are some activities that can prepare your body for a regular workout:

Walking.

This is probably the simplest way to ease into an exercise program after delivery. It may not seem like much, but it's an excellent way to get regular daily physical activity.

How to: Start with a simple stroll and gradually move up to power walks. You can carry your baby along in a pack; the extra weight will boost the benefits of your walks. I recommend walking backward or in a zigzag pattern to keep your muscles curious.

Note: Do not include your baby in these variations of walking.

Deep belly breathing with abdominal contractions.

This is the easiest activity ever for new moms. You can even do it a few hours after delivery. It will relax your muscles and is a great way to strengthen and tone your belly.

How to: Sit upright and take a deep breath on your belly. Contract as tightly as possible when you breathe in and relax when you exhale. Try for 5-10 minutes at first, then gradually increase how long you do it.

Kneeling pelvic tilt.

This activity can help you strengthen your abs and tone your tummy. It also reduces back pain.

How to: Get on all fours, with toes touching the ground behind you. Keep your arms straight from your shoulder line and palms flat on the floor. Relax and straighten your back; don't curve or arch. When you inhale, jerk your buttocks to the front, tilt your pelvis, and rotate your pubic bone upward. Do this on a count of three, then release.

Kegels.

This is a classic exercise that's good for toning bladder muscles. It can help to reduce the risks of incontinence after childbirth. The longer your Kegels, the better control you'll have over leaks caused by laughing, sneezing, or picking up your baby.

How to: Start when you pee in the bathroom. Contract and hold your muscles until the pee temporarily stops coming. Then, release and let the stream flow. Make a mental note of how you did that, then repeat with the same muscles when you aren't peeing. Do three times daily and ten Kegels per session.

Head lifts, shoulder lifts, curl-ups.

These three movements can help strengthen your back muscles if practiced regularly. They also burn calories and tone the abs.

How to: For head lifts, lie flat on your back and keep your arms by your side. Ensure your lower back is flush to the surface, keep your feet flat on the floor, and bend your knees. Inhale and relax your belly. And when you exhale, lift your head off the floor gently. Then, lower back down as you inhale.

Once you're good at this, do shoulder lifts following the same steps. But this time, lift your head and shoulder off the floor. You may fold your hands behind your head to make it easier.

Move on to curl-ups when you can do ten shoulder lifts at once. Follow the same steps, but lift your entire torso and reach toward your knees this time. Wait for 2-5 seconds before lowering your torso back down.

Remember to breathe. Inhale when you relax and exhale when you lift.

Other exercises you can try include:

- Single arm rows
- Wall push-ups
- Wall plank rotations

- Cat cows
- Wall sits
- Quadrupled leg lifts
- Bridges
- Supine leg lifts

You can watch Youtube videos for a step-by-step guide on how to practice each of these activities.

I want to conclude this chapter by telling you about a new mom I met a few years back. While I don't want to put her in the spotlight as she requested, I'd like to call her Mary.

Mary was one of those new moms excited to start exercising after giving birth. She wanted to lose the extra pounds as soon as possible because she valued being fit. And to make the process easier and faster, Mary started following a diet from a friend.

Everything was good – she was starting to burn the fat and get into shape. Unfortunately, Mary's newborn got an ear infection after a few months. This made her exercise and diet routine take a downward spiral. She couldn't keep up. This went on for some months, but thankfully, she was able to get back on her routine.

If you're wondering why I'm telling you about Mary, it's to emphasize the importance of consistency. Life challenges are inevitable, especially for a new mom. And when they come, remember to take just 5 minutes of your day to do some stretches – no matter what.

Though it may sound too good to be true, these simple acts of self-care and self-compassion discussed in this chapter can positively impact your life. And the harder you make them a lifestyle, the bigger the benefits. That, of course, makes it easier to get back on top of your life.

3

SIMPLIFYING LIFE AND ROUTINES

"You have to leave the house every now and then! You need fresh air and direct sunlight. It really helps."

— TAMARA SYKES

A few weeks into your life as a new mom, you'll feel like your home has been overrun with baby things and clutter. This is a feeling most new mothers are familiar with. It's okay if life feels chaotic.

The question is, how do you simplify your routines and life in general? You want to take care of your newborn, but you also want to sit in your favorite chair, read your favorite book, and drink a hot cup of coffee.

Perhaps, you fancy the idea of having a friend over for tea or whatever. You don't want your home to look like it's been taken over by a clutter of baby things and other stuff – much of which you don't even need. Before the arrival of your newborn, you may have been used to a perfect routine. Now, everything is all over the place.

In this chapter, you will discover how to bring peace and calm back to your home. More importantly, there are tips on successfully creating a new routine to manage your time better. Finally, you will learn how to declutter and organize your home so that you feel comfortable and proud.

Let's get to it.

TIME FOR A REALISTIC LOOK AT INVENTORY

The internet is awash with lists of "essential" and "must-have" items to stock up on for a newborn baby. If it's your first time, you naturally want to do everything possible to be a "good" mom.

At this stage, the nesting hormones are running wild. And when these collide with first-time jitters, salespeople can take advantage of your apprehensiveness to convince you about items you MUST buy to be a good mother.

Of course, you want to be an ideal parent, so create a checklist and head to your nearest baby warehouse to buy as many items as possible. You aren't alone in this, as many new moms believe they must do everything right to prepare for their little bundle of joy.

I wish I had people who were honest with me about what I needed and, most importantly, what I didn't need when I had my first child. Then, I could have saved a lot of money and time, avoided stress, and prevented the clutter that clogged up my home after my baby's birth.

We live in a materialistic and consumerist society that convinces us that being a good parent depends on how often we want to tap on our credit card.

Baby things are some of the biggest contributors to clutter. Apart from what you get yourself, everyone seems to want to prove that they're a better friend or grandparent by gifting you a bunch of stuff your baby doesn't need.

You'd be surprised at how fast babies grow, meaning their needs are ever-changing. Therefore, it is unlikely that your baby would end up using the mountain of gifts and stuff everyone gets for them.

Clutter hurts the mental health of new moms. It not only impairs your ability to cope while dealing with postpartum sleeplessness but also makes it harder to adjust to the demands of your adorable little one.

To help you reduce the possibility of clutter as much as possible, I have carefully created a list of things your baby doesn't need – things your infant can get by just fine without. This list is based on my experience and other moms I have spoken to over the years.

Note that the purpose of this list isn't to judge you or your choices but to help take the burden off your mind and wallet.

Without further ado, let's get to the list.

- **Newborn-sized clothes**

It's normal to be tempted by the allure of newborn-sized clothes – after all, they are always so cute. Unfortunately, your infant will most likely outgrow them in no time. The average American newborn weighs 7.5 pounds at birth, whereas these clothes only fit newborns up to seven pounds.

I suggest going for clothes for babies between 0 and 3 months. These fit babies up to 12 pounds and are just as cute as newborn-sized clothes.

- **A Nursery**

Contrary to what Hollywood tells us, babies don't need a dedicated room. Nurseries are quite expensive to set up and also unnecessary. Children specialists have always reiterated how important it is for newborn babies to remain close to their primary parent all the time, including at nighttime. Some recommend that babies stay in the same room as their parents for the first 6-12 months at the very least.

- **Crib bumpers**

Crib bumpers may be cute, but they are only great in theory. As a mommy, you want to protect your newborn from knocking into the hard walls of their crib. However, crib bumpers are a suffocation threat to babies, especially newborns.

The American Academy of Pediatrics warns new moms against using bumpers, including the mesh versions. So, take them off your checklist.

- **Shoes**

At this stage, your newborn isn't moving or going anywhere. They can't even walk, making shoes one of infants' most unnecessary purchases. Another thing is babies can't keep those tiny kicks on.

Suppose you're worried your little one might get cold toes. In that case, you can get some thick baby socks or booties with snaps. That'll make sure the booties stay on instead of getting kicked off.

- **Changing table**

This isn't a complete "don't buy" item, but you can leave it off the list if you're cash-strapped or don't have enough space in your home. One thing about babies is that you can change their diapers anywhere. You only need a couple of changing pads and can use the couch, bed, or floor as a changing surface.

- **Bassinet**

The bassinets are cozy but pretty pricey as well. Many cost up to a hundred dollars, and there are significantly more expensive ones. So, you might want to take a bassinet off your list. If you're still considering buying a bassinet, remember you'll have to stash it away for three months max. Plus, your baby may not sleep in it all that much.

- **Infant bathtub**

Your baby won't be a newborn for over three months, so buying a newborn-sized bathtub is ridiculous. You can easily get by without this. But if you want a bathtub for your baby, consider getting a full-sized baby bathtub – especially one with a sling for infant use.

- **Baby blankets**

You will surely get this from your friends, neighbors, coworkers, and relatives. As such, there's no point buying baby blankets with your money because you will get plenty anyway. Trust me!

Other items your baby does not need include:

- A baby brush
- Toys
- Designer pram
- Designer baby bag
- Teddies
- Baby jewelry and headbands
- Ribbons, bows, buttons, and other fiddly items
- Walkers or jolly jumpers
- Dummies

If you doubt whether your newborn will need some of these non-essential items, wait until he or she is born, and purchase them then.

TOP TIPS FOR DECLUTTERING THE HOME AND WHY

Let's face it – you are probably staring at a pile of clutter as you're reading this. You often hear that it's important for moms to declutter and organize the home. And you know you should, but you aren't sure where to start. How do you even find time to declutter your entire home? Sounds like a lot of work, and you're busy with the baby.

The mere idea of letting go of things isn't exciting, but clearing clutter out of your home is an important activity you must regularly engage in as a form of self-care. It can have such a huge impact on your mental well-being. Believe me when I say regular decluttering will change your life.

Clutter is more than a pile of stuff sitting around and gathering dust. It includes anything you don't love or require. It can be physical, emotional, or mental. Clutter takes on different forms, and all can hold you back from achieving peace in your home.

Living in a cluttered environment triggers stress, anxiety, depression, and sometimes insomnia – all of which negatively impact your mental health. It distracts you and takes peace out of your home and life.

Additionally, living with clutter means you waste more time looking for things and cleaning your home. These can be frustrating and exhausting when added to your busy schedule as a new mom.

In short, decluttering your living space will make cleaning easier, help you find things faster, improve your physical and mental well-being, and help you achieve tranquility in your personal space.

Generally, new moms feel overwhelmed and preoccupied with the baby. There is no shame in admitting that. It's okay if you don't know how to start decluttering because you're stressed and overwhelmed.

I want to take some of that stress off you by sharing the easiest decluttering ideas you'll find anywhere. Trust me; I know finding time for the simplest tasks as a new mom can be hard. You may think there's no time to declutter, but doing it now will buy you plenty of time to invest in other productive activities.

Once decluttering becomes a part of your routine, it will become simple and better. So, here are nine steps you can take to begin making decluttering a lifestyle.

1. Make a plan.

First, choose a day for decluttering and the time of day that works best for you. Second, always set a timer for 5-10 minutes at a stretch. Third, choose a particular area to declutter and stick to that area within your assigned timeframe. Trying to tackle multiple areas at once always results in more piles. It's much better to focus on one at a time. Even if you have to spend a week or more decluttering just one room, do it.

2. Create a checklist.

A checklist will help you to set your priorities straight. Plus, you can check tasks off the list as you complete them. Begin by listing which parts of your home need to be decluttered the most, then work your way down gradually. Making a decluttering checklist will help you stay on track.

3. Purge your clothes and baby clothing.

I consider this the best way to start decluttering. Purging your home of your belongings is an effective way to eliminate plenty of unwanted stuff at once. So, go through every area in your home and find things you don't need or use to get rid of. Include things that are taking up space without serving any purpose.

Collect items you haven't used in six months or more because you most likely don't need them. Do not keep things due to sentiment – you can easily store them away until your baby is older.

4. Make a storage system.

After decluttering, you have to think of where everything will go. This is why you need an efficient and functional storage system that aligns with your needs and lifestyle. I suggest getting quality storage baskets and bins, then labeling them to know what goes where at all times. Creating a storage system can help you keep clutter from piling up again.

5. Don't stop decluttering.

Getting rid of clutter must be an ongoing practice. The purpose is to eliminate stuff and create space and time while ensuring the piles never return. Once you complete the major part of decluttering your home, you should create an ongoing plan so you don't have to do it all over again.

6. Make a donation box.

This is something you must have at all times. When you find something the family no longer needs, toss it in the donation box. You can throw away clothes, shoes, toys, old books, etc. It's an effective way to keep clutter from piling again.

7. Make an annual decluttering plan for toys.

When it comes to toys, you should declutter at least two times a year. I recommend making it two weekends in the first half and second half of the year, respectively.

8. Eliminate clutter hotspots.

Some parts of your home may be the subconsciously designated clutter spots – the kitchen counter, nightstand, coffee table, dresser top, etc. Your hotspot could be your closets, as these are some of the biggest clutter causes. A storage system can help you get rid of these clutter hotspots.

9. Do not create a "maybe" pile.

Sometimes, people are undecided about getting rid of certain stuff, so they make a "maybe" pile. This is not a good idea as it makes decluttering an unfinished task with a new type of pile sitting around in your home,

If you start making those little changes now, the difference will be visible in just a few months. So, set the time and get to decluttering your home now. And don't forget to enlist your family's help throughout the process.

ADAPTING TO A NEW ROUTINE THAT SUITS YOU BOTH

Babies thrive on routine, and the best way to take control of your time is to create one that works for your baby and you. Many new parents find that adapting to a daily routine makes their life much easier.

Creating a routine is as simple as observing when your infant likes to eat, sleep, and play and then building a schedule. Learning about your newborn's feeding and sleeping habits will take a while, so don't expect to create a routine in the first few weeks.

Having a routine can be incredibly helpful. For one, it makes detecting the reason for your baby's cries much easier. If you have a scheduled feeding or sleeping time, you can rule out hunger or sleep when the baby cries. Additionally, a routine ensures your newborn is well-fed at all times. Your baby will acclimate to the schedule, reducing the need for snacks throughout the day.

Humans enjoy the comfort predictability brings – and babies aren't excluded. If you create the right routine, your newborn will be well-fed, well-rested, and content when they aren't asleep.

Here are simple tips to help you find the perfect schedule for you and your infant.

- **Follow a pattern to differentiate between night and day.**

Babies can't tell the difference between night and day at first. That is why your newborn could sleep for long stretches during the day and stay awake at night. Teaching your baby this difference is vital to creating the right routine.

Simple habits can communicate this to them. Change the baby's clothes to bedtime clothes and again in the morning. This tells the baby when one-day ends and another begins. Also, keep your home bright and loud during the day; but quiet and dim at nighttimes.

Night feeds should be quieter and calmer than day feeds. Speak to the baby calmly at nighttime, reduce background noise, and make the room as dark as possible. It helps to reduce how much you talk during the nighttime.

These simple habits teach the baby that daytime is playtime and nighttime is for sleeping.

- **Be consistent.**

Consistency is non-negotiable. It's best to be consistent daily to allow your newborn to get used to the routine. It's the only way to help them understand that certain things happen at certain times.

- **Read the baby's clues.**

Babies give clues when they want to eat, sleep, or play. Let your baby guide you to the perfect routine. Watch for patterns so that you can anticipate their needs. Make a note of when the baby tends to get hungry, tired, or ready to play. For example, if you notice cues that your newborn is hungry, feed them immediately.

Remember that it'll take time and patience to fully learn what your baby wants at different points during the day.

- **Adjust the routine to suit your baby's age.**

Once you fall into a predictable pattern, it won't take time before you have to change your routine again. You must adjust the routine as your baby ages to accommodate their growth.

A typical routine may look like this:

7 am - 7:30 am – wake up and feed
8:00 am – nap time
10:00 am – feed, diaper change, play
10:40 am – nap time
12:30 pm – feed, diaper change, play
1:10 pm – nap time
3:00 pm – feed, diaper change, play
3:40 pm – nap time
6:00 pm – feed, diaper change, play
6:30 pm – cat nap
7:20 - 8:00 pm – diaper change, bedtime
8:30 pm – cluster feed
11:00 pm – feed, swaddle, put to bed

Then, when your newborn wakes up at any point during the night, feed them again. On average, this may be every three hours.

GETTING ORGANIZED WITH BRAIN FOG

Pregnancy-induced brain fog is real. It can be frustrating and stays long after your baby is born. You may forget doctor appointments, where you left the keys, what you're at the store for – and even your baby's vital documents.

Having a baby comes with plenty of new responsibilities, and pregnancy-induced forgetfulness doesn't make that easier. It's easy to forget about essential documents that must be safely filed away for your newborn.

Brain fog is normal and common among pregnant women. Even with a great organization or multitasking skills, you may still struggle with concentrating or remembering things. So, the first thing you must do is file your newborn's vital documents in a folder.

Here's what to include in the baby folder:

- Birth certificate
- Social security card
- Immunization record
- Doctor visits
- Feeding and sleep schedule
- Insurance paperwork
- Keepsakes
- Milestones

The good news is brain fog isn't forever. You'll regain total recall long before your "senior moments" begin. In the meantime, these tips will help you manage pregnancy forgetfulness effectively.

- **Take regular deep breaths.** Don't be hard on yourself. Stress can exert your mind, making your memory even foggier. Take deep breaths now and then to relax and calm your mind.
- **Jot things down.** If you need to make a phone call, ask your doctor a question, buy certain things, or take medication – write it down in a note. You might want to keep a pen and notepad close in an easy-to-find spot, like your purse, bathroom, or car. Keep your notepad in the most obvious place so you can remember easily.
- **Make a backup system.** Delegate tasks to other family members to reduce the number of things you must remember. Let them serve as your backup system; it'll make a difference.
- **Use a reminder app.** The calendar app on your phone is a great tool for reminding yourself of things to be done. It can help keep you organized.
- **Be ready.** The fog will be there in the first few weeks or months after delivery. And it'll be complicated by postpartum fatigue and insomnia, so prepare yourself.

Again, go easy on yourself!

FINDING YOUR SUPPORT SYSTEM

A strong support system and social connections are two essential things every mother needs. But we often convince ourselves that seeking help from friends and family is a sign of weakness. Many new moms believe it indicates they can't cope with their new role as a parent. This is untrue.

Your family can help around the home; friends can make you laugh when you're at your wit's end; and the community can assist with vital resources in their own way. There's nothing quite like having a group of mothers familiar with your struggles and experiences.

I cannot overstate the importance of having a healthy group of people to support you through this major transition, especially when considering the exhaustion of caring for a newborn.

So, here are five ways to seek out and build a healthy support system.

1. **Family:** Relatives can improve your physical, mental, and emotional well-being simply by showing up and helping with things where you are falling behind. For example, your parents might help prepare a meal or do the dishes occasionally. And sometimes, your siblings can

help monitor the baby while you nap. Everyone can play a role.

2. **Friends:** Good friends are a key element of a baby support network. You can lean on them for laughter, camaraderie, and help with your workload. Let your friends know you'll reach out to them whenever you need assistance. Good pals will consider it an honor to help in their way.

3. **Mentors:** If you have people in your current social network whom you admire their parenting style – friends, coworkers, relatives, or friends of friends – you can reach out to them for guidance on this new journey. They can even help you with links to communities and social groups for new moms.

4. **Community:** Many towns offer new parents assistance through visitation services, diaper drives, and mommy-and-me outings. You can use these to establish a community-wide support network for your newborn. Your local library may also offer resources and activities to connect you with people and programs to make your journey easier.

5. **Online:** Not everyone lives close to family. Some stay in urban areas where it's much harder to find support. If this applies to you, check online support groups so you can find a community.

I know of a friend who took time to declutter a home a few weeks before and after birth and donated things she no longer needed to local groups. Not only did this act of kindness improve her self-esteem and emotional well-being, but it also allowed her to make new friends and build a support network in a place where she didn't have that many family and friends.

Decluttering and organizing can make you feel on top of things – which you are. They instill a peace of mind and a sense of achievement. Look around your decluttered and organized home, and you'll feel immensely happy.

But there will be some emotional roller coaster along the way. In the next chapter, we'll discuss the role of emotional intelligence in self-care.

4

GETTING HONEST ABOUT HOW YOU ARE FEELING

"You do not need to suffer in silence or feel ashamed. Our babies need us to be healthy during a time when we are overwhelmed the most."

— BRITTANY WILLOW MAYER

Regardless of how much you prepared or looked forward to starting life as a mom, you will face some highs and lows in the first few months. One thing you may not be prepared for is the amount of emotional ups and downs that happens after your baby's birth.

Certain emotional problems may arise after having your baby. Many refer to these problems as postpartum depression, but this is misleading. Postpartum depression is a diagnosable condition that happens to some women after birth. In contrast, the emotional rollercoaster I'm talking about is something all new moms struggle with postnatal.

This chapter explores the range of emotions you may experience in the first few weeks or months after childbirth. Even though your hormones will be dictating your emotions wildly, it's still important for you to become skilled at recognizing your feelings and why they are there.

We will also discuss common emotional triggers and the best strategies for regulating these emotions when they become overwhelming. So, let's begin by looking at the most common emotions new moms experience.

COMMON EMOTIONAL PROBLEMS IN NEW MOMS

Becoming a mom is the peak of fulfillment for many women. It can mean your dream has come true. During pregnancy, you may love the feeling of your baby moving inside you. Then, there is the sense of achievement many feel when they give birth. That sense of wonder when you touch, watch, smell, or play with your baby.

However, not all new moms feel that overwhelming sense of love immediately. Sometimes, the positive feelings associated with motherhood are accompanied by worry, fear, frustration, anxiety, guilt, and a sense of loss.

You might think:

- What if I'm not a good mom?
- Will I make many mistakes?
- What if I make a mistake that affects my baby forever?

These can evoke difficult emotions and negative thoughts that may be fueled by lack of sleep, worries about the birth, and anxieties about how you're doing as a parent. You might feel you can't share these thoughts and feelings out of shame or embarrassment.

Several factors contribute to the rise of emotional problems in postpartum women – from biological to social. They increase feelings of stress, anxiety, or depression. Most women can cope with a few emotional difficulties, but multiple problems can be overwhelming for anyone.

Emotional risk factors include:

- Anxiety before or during pregnancy
- Having severe baby blues
- Having a negative outlook on life
- Low self-esteem and self-criticism
- Feeling alone during your birth process

Here are some feelings that may arise as a result of these emotional risk factors. Know that they're completely normal – everyone deals with a few of these at some point.

Sadness

After my first delivery, I wouldn't stop crying. I was awash with a sense of sadness. Was I sad to be a mom? Of course not. I soon found out that it was normal for pregnant or new moms to cry over seemingly little things.

You might find your eyes welling up because you couldn't change a diaper well on your first try – or because you misplaced your phone and couldn't find it quickly enough.

It's not unusual for new moms to deal with intermittent feelings of sadness and emotional hypersensitivity. These are common manifestations of the baby blues, which only last a few days or weeks.

Fear

Being a mother comes with a new range of fears, even for women who were never the worrying type before birth. From minor to complex fears, the feelings can be over- whelming in the first few months of motherhood.

When I had my daughter, I feared being alone with her. I feared I wouldn't know what to do with her. Would I underfeed or overfeed her? How do I soothe her? How do I know if she needs something?

That fear that you won't be able to care for your child properly because you don't know anything about parenting is something every mom is familiar with. It may be new to you, but it is familiar to millions of women who have been in your situation before.

You are not the first mother to have these fears – including the irrational ones – and you definitely won't be the last.

Anger

Not all mothers admit this, but many experience anger in the early days after delivery. You might be angry at yourself for not knowing how to breastfeed or at the world because you can't get the baby to stop crying.

This is especially common with moms who set high standards for themselves or lean toward perfectionism. However, it could be a sign of postpartum mood disorder if anger is severe and persistent.

Anxiety

It's normal to feel on edge several weeks after giving birth. You may be tense, anxious, and easily startled. You will find it quite unsettling if you've never felt this way. But be rest assured that it's a common emotional problem with new moms.

During the first few weeks after my daughter's birth, I felt like I had suffered from anxiety attacks all my life. I wasn't sleeping, worrying a lot, and feeling extremely over-whelmed. But the anxieties eventually disappeared as I adjusted to life as a mom.

Emotional hypersensitivity

A common feeling after childbirth is hypersensitivity to everyone's emotions. You may feel deeply affected by everyone and everything. Watching a sad movie could have you weeping like you were the main character.

It's normal for emotions to be all over the place. This doesn't necessarily mean you have postnatal depression or a mood disorder. It's all baby blues – but if it persists for over two weeks, you should speak to your doctor.

As I said, these feelings are all too common and normal. So, it's important to not be hard on yourself. Consider the first few weeks post-delivery as a learning curve for you and your newborn.

LET'S TAKE THE HORMONES OUT OF THE PICTURE

The emotional highs and lows after giving birth are typically caused by hormonal changes. After delivery, estrogen and progesterone production significantly decline, triggering mood swings.

For some women, the hormones produced in the thyroid gland decrease sharply, causing exhaustion and mild depression. These feelings can be further complicated if a new mom doesn't eat well or get enough sleep.

Baby blues and emotional issues happen hand-in-hand. If you are anxious about caring for your newborn or worried about how having the baby will change your life, these can cause feelings of sadness or depression.

You may be at increased risk for sadness if you've been depressed at any time in your life or if you felt depressed during another pregnancy.

But even though hormones may be the primary reason for emotional struggles, you shouldn't just blame hormonal changes. It's best to address the underlying issues.

For example, suppose you feel lonely after childbirth, which makes you sad. In that case, you can seek other new moms to share your feelings with and hang out together. Having someone to talk to about your experiences as a new mom is incredibly important. Having someone to laugh with can relieve anxiety, sadness, or isolation.

So, check out your local mom and baby groups online. Also, don't let being a new parent stop you from catching up with old friends.

As you navigate these emotions, know that feeling overwhelmed is normal. I would be worried if any postpartum woman told me they weren't overwhelmed by their new life. There's always so much to do after having a baby, and changes are overwhelming by default.

The main thing is to be kind to yourself as you adjust to your new reality and responsibilities. You'll need a lot of time for this to happen – don't feel bad, though. Take every opportunity to remind yourself that you've got this.

Additionally, exhaustion is inevitable when you're a new parent. It's practically impossible not to feel exhausted. Just try and rest as well as possible whenever you can.

Even if you don't feel like it, one emotion that will be a constant is the feeling of joy. Being a mom is a wonderful experience. You may be surprised at how often feelings of happiness over your little one will well up inside you.

Whenever this happens, embrace the feeling and let the love and warmth flow.

THE SELF-CARE BRAIN DUMP

Mom's brain is real and very much so. You probably know this now because your mind has been a mess since you had your child. Many people don't know this, but the concept of a "mom brain" is recognized psychologically.

Studies show that women's brains physically change to make us more sensitive to our kids' needs. Basically, your brain rewires itself to promote a sense of caring and nurturing. Sadly, this has downsides, such as increased sensitivity and memory interference.

That's when you start to feel intensely anxious because you forgot something and can't remember it, no matter how hard you try. Or you try to do something and have no idea where or how to begin.

Being a mom means you have lots of things to do other than just parenting. You could be running a business, side hustle, or managing your home, family, finances, or career. Obviously, this is all a lot, so it's inevitable that you'd feel overwhelmed.

You know when it feels like your head might explode because a gazillion thoughts are floating inside at once? Thoughts about your baby, home, family, partner, finances, etc., and you can't identify a starting point. Every woman knows that feeling. But not everyone is familiar with a psychological self-care technique called a "brain dump."

A brain dump is a highly effective tool for freeing your mind and body of emotional tension. Doing a brain dump is as simple as getting a pen and notepad and emptying your mind for as long as you want.

Mental self-care caters to the mind. It is vital for improving your mental health. And it involves engaging in activities that foster a clear mind and positive outlook while decreasing stress. A brain dump is one of the ways you can engage in mental self-care.

You can take a structured or unstructured approach to do a brain dump. It all depends on you, what works for you, and your needs and preferences. No matter the approach you take, a brain dump should do the following:

- Ground you in the present.
- Reduce overwhelming feelings.
- Decrease feelings of stress and anxiety.
- Declutter your mind.
- Create mental energy.
- Provide guidance for going about your day.

Depending on your needs, some ways to structure your brain dump exist. You may address different areas of your life on different pages of your notepad. For instance: page 1, baby; page 2, family; page 3, home tasks, etc.

I usually alternate between mind mapping, listing, or writing down everything inside my head at once.

To get started, you can write down the following in different lists:

- You must make upcoming appointments (set reminders on your calendar).
- Decluttering and cleaning ideas (parts of your home that are disorganized and need deep cleaning).
- To-do list for the week.
- Goals for the week or month.
- Pending bills.
- Grocery shopping (items you're out of).
- Things you or your family, including the newborn, need.
- Meal plan lists.
- Books you want to read.
- Movies or shows you want to watch.
- Ideas for your side hustle or business.
- Self-care routines to follow weekly.
- Your thoughts and feelings about any situation or problem.
- Date night ideas with your partner.

Brain dumps are a form of psychological self-care that cater to your mind. A decluttered mind is focused, ready, and motivated. So, make this a daily or weekly activity to start seeing immediate results.

The more brain dumps you do, the less forgetful you'll become and the less anxious you'll feel with time.

HOW YOUR EMOTIONAL INTELLIGENCE WILL HELP BABY

There is a growing appreciation for emotional intelligence skills. Parenting would be significantly easier if we could all find the balance between head and heart. But many parents find it hard to attune to their kids' emotions.

Dealing with this requires boosting our EQ, i.e., emotional quotient, i.e., the ability to be aware of your emotions and others and manage them effectively. This isn't as simple as it sounds, but it's something every parent can learn if we put in the work.

One thing we've established so far in this chapter is that motherhood is characterized by overwhelming emotions. Just so many feelings are involved in the process, from beginning to end. Yet, we barely take time to process these feelings. In worse cases, we may ignore or suppress our feelings instead of addressing them.

As a mother, boosting your emotional intelligence not only helps you but your kids as well. The good news is that while some are more predisposed to emotional intelligence than others, it's something we all learn growing up. No one is born with emotional intelligence, but we can all learn the skills.

I could argue that the greatest benefit of emotional intelligence is its impact on mental health. Laying a foundation of EI skills can positively impact the developing areas of your baby's brain that contribute to psychological well-being.

Babies develop within the dynamic of their relationships, particularly with their primary caregiver. Your infant's daily experiences with you influence the wiring of neural pathways. Emotionally attuned, responsive, and empathetic interactions between children and their caregivers or other significant adults stimulate the creation of neural connections and pathways.

Consistent positive experiences with you, the family, and other adults help establish a healthy patterning of your baby's brain, influencing who they become before they can pronounce their name.

Approaching your interactions with your kid in an emotionally intelligent way:

- Boosts their self-esteem
- Helps to develop empathy
- Builds self-regulation skills
- Increases capacity for critical thinking and problem-solving
- Strengthens character and moral development

As your child grows, their behavior, mood, and exhaustion can affect your ability to understand their emotions. So, you must work on boosting your emotional intelligence by building these five skills.

1. **Self-awareness:** You need to be emotionally self-aware. Self-awareness involves recognizing what you're feeling in the moment so you can evaluate your emotion and respond appropriately. The more you practice becoming aware of your feelings and moods and how they affect people around you, the more your emotional intelligence increases.

2. **Self-regulation:** This skill is about controlling your emotional responses. It means thinking before you react to a frustrating or upsetting situation. It's all about learning to redirect potentially destructive feelings, moods, or impulses.

3. **Motivation:** Some days, the only reward for your efforts as a mother is the innate sense that you're doing your best. This is intrinsic motivation and is a great way to maintain optimism in the face of setbacks.

4. **Empathy:** This means putting yourself in your child's metaphorical shoes when dealing with a situation. It's about considering your child's emotional makeup so you can better cater to their needs.

5. **Social skills:** This EI skill involves building a rapport with others so you can manage conflict and build teamwork.

For you, building these emotional intelligence skills can help to:

- **Express yourself better.**

Emotional intelligence isn't something you learn once and remember forever. Just as you'd have to train your kids to express their feelings at different points, you must also equip yourself to do the same.

- **Manage stress.**

Undeniably, motherhood is a stressful period. You cannot completely control your stress level, but emotional intelligence can help you manage it. This begins with self-awareness and evaluation.

First, you learn to identify your stress triggers. Then, evaluate how you respond to stress and modify your responses accordingly. Regulating and evaluating your responses to stressful situations can help boost self-regulation skills.

- **Increase empathy.**

Boosting your EQ will help you empathize with your kids more. Managing intense emotions isn't easy; children experience these emotions more intensely than adults. So, the more you practice your EQ skills, the easier it becomes to empathize with your children's temper tantrums. It's helpful when your kids see how you react in overwhelming situations, handle setbacks, and manage your emotions.

You can't always get it right with your emotions, but learning to identify triggers can make it much easier.

HAVE YOU GOT NEW TRIGGERS?

You experience various emotions, from anxiety to frustration, unease, joy, and excitement on any given day. Usually, these emotions are tied to specific events, such as seeing your partner. But when you become a mom, it seems like you're constantly experiencing emotions that aren't tied to any situation (trigger) – except this isn't right. Every emotional experience is tied to a trigger.

A trigger is anything – thought, memory, event, or experience – that evokes an intense emotional response, despite your current mood. If you were quite familiar with your triggers before childbirth, you'd be surprised at how quickly new ones spring up after.

Knowing your triggers and how best to deal with them is one of the foundations of developing emotional intelligence.

Almost every mom has distinct emotional triggers, which often look slightly different from mom to mom. Generally, they include other people's words or actions, your child's behavior, reminders of unpleasant memories, or uncomfortable topics.

Common triggers for new moms include:

- Helplessness
- Loss of control
- Criticism
- Feeling alone or unwanted
- Feeling too needed
- Challenged beliefs
- Feeling unjustly treated
- Loss of independence

The list of things that can trigger you is never-ending, but these are some of the most common among new mothers.

Identifying new triggers can be complicated, but I have simplified it in these three steps.

1. Pay attention to your body.

Notice what happens in your body when you're overwhelmed by an intense emotion. Is your heart racing? Are you breathing faster than usual? Are your muscles tense? Examining your physiological responses makes it easier to identify the trigger.

2. Take a few steps back.

Once you know your emotion, take a few steps back to see how you got to that situation. For example, what were you doing right before the emotion sprung up? Did you feel it coming at any particular moment?

Remember that it can be anything, so explore everything that happened until that point.

3. Repeat

It's fine if you can't identify your trigger on the first try. Repeat these steps anytime you have an intense emotional reaction, and you'll get better each time.

Here's how to manage triggers:

- Acknowledge the emotion.
- Feel the physical manifestations of that emotion.
- Put your feelings into words.
- Own the feeling – remind yourself that having that feeling is okay.
- Deliberately change how you respond to the emotion.

Identifying and managing your triggers may take time, but you'll get there.

EMOTIONAL REGULATION FOR A HAPPIER LIFE

When building your self-regulation skills, taking an integrated approach works wonders. So, we're about to look at some strategies you can combine to effectively regulate your emotions. Find which works best for you.

1. Calm your nervous system.

The autonomic nervous system controls emotional dysregulation. So, calming your nervous system can be a great strategy for regulating your emotions. To soothe your nervous system, you can:

➤ Take a cold shower.
➤ Listen to soothing music.
➤ Hold an ice cube in your hand.
➤ Place your hand on your heart and count the beats.

2. Accept how you feel.

Challenging your emotions at the moment never works. So, when you're emotionally overwhelmed, don't question what you're feeling. Instead, accept the feeling and reframe it. Ask yourself:

➤ What can I do right now in this moment?
➤ What tools are at my disposal?
➤ Where, how, and with whom can I feel safer in this moment?

Accepting your emotions may help you calm down in the moment.

3. TIPP

This is an emotional regulation strategy that entails the following:

➤ **Temperature:** Intense emotions can cause your temperature to rise, and you can reduce the intensity by lowering your temp. Consider splashing cold water on your face to induce a relaxed sensation.

➤ **Intense exercise:** Walking, jogging, or running can help you cool off and feel better. A quick cardio session is one of the best ways to regulate your feelings.

➤ **Paced breathing:** Inhaling and exhaling slower than usual is a great way to calm yourself down when heated. Pacing your breath allows your mind to pause and think.

➤ **Paired muscle relaxation:** Intense emotions typically cause sore muscles. Deal with this by tensing your affected muscle and inhaling for 5 seconds. Then, exhale for 7 seconds and release the tension in your affected muscle. It'll help you feel better.

4. ACES

Another emotional regulation strategy that requires using your emotional intelligence skills. It is characterized by four things:

➤ **Awareness:** Understand the source of your emotion to learn to control it.

➤ **Component:** Accept your feeling as a part of you, but know you can't control it. You can only control your response to that emotion.

➤ **Explore:** Try to understand your emotion and find ways to express it healthily.

➤ **Shift:** Choose whether to shift your emotional response after understanding the root.

5. Distancing

This strategy involves distancing yourself from the emotion as if you're someone observing it from afar. Do not immerse yourself in the feeling. Instead, look at it from someone else's perspective. That way, you won't lose yourself to negative feelings. Even if you do feel bad, you do not feel as bad.

Another approach is temporal distancing, which involves looking at your emotion or the trigger event from a different point in time. This can dampen the emotional intensity by showing you that negative feelings aren't permanent.

6. Consider the story you're telling yourself

Think about how you're interpreting the triggering situation. Is it the only explanation, or there are other explanations? This strategy encourages you to look at your emotions from different perspectives to reach a reasonable conclusion.

7. Choose how to respond

No matter how intense or overwhelming an emotion is, you can choose how to respond. Next time you are in an emotionally intense situation, be deliberate about your response. Choose how you want to respond.

Remember to be consistent with these strategies to develop your emotional regulation skills for a happier life.

I once introduced a friend to deep breathing to regulate her emotions, but she was one of those who believed the benefits to be an old wives' tale. It was hard, but I convinced her to give it a try for at least a week. If she didn't see a difference in her life, I would stop propagating the gospel of deep breathing. Of course, that never happened because she realized it was everything and more. And that's why I'm here spreading the gospel to you too. Give it a try today!

Our emotions are ruled by our thoughts, and our thoughts by our emotions. The good news is that when emotions are under control, it's easier to identify negative thought patterns and work toward reframing them to be more productive.

5

CALMING YOUR CRITICAL INNER MOM VOICE

> *"I just keep telling myself through all of the phases, "it's not forever, it just feels like it."*

— MICHELLE GREELEY

The overwhelming responsibility of caring for a newborn often triggers a heightened state of vigilance in mothers. Sometimes, this creates confusion, especially for new moms. At every turn, you believe something bad is looming.

Afraid of accidentally dropping your infant, you hold them tightly everywhere you go. Out of fear, you stay awake at night to watch your baby as they sleep soundly. And when you fall asleep, you dream that your negligence has somehow caused harm to the infant.

Then, you have the critical inner voice – a pattern of dysfunctional thoughts and beliefs about yourself and others. It is a series of thoughts experienced within your mind. Your critical inner voice is self-destructive and discourages you from acting in your best interest. It's always there telling you something will happen to the baby if you don't do this or that.

Think of the critical inner voice as an internal enemy that attacks every area of your life, including your intimate relationship, self-esteem and confidence, personal accomplishments, and motherhood.

We all normally have a critical inner voice. Still, when you become a mother, that voice amplifies and threatens to take over your mind. It dictates your mood, feelings, thoughts, and actions – and you don't even realize it.

Your critical inner voice undermines your positive feelings about motherhood, fostering self-doubt, self-criticism, distrust, self-denial, and an aversion to goal-driven activities. Common "voices" include thoughts like, "I am stupid," "I am a bad mother," or "I am not as good at parenting as other people."

Many moms experience voices about their kids, such as "He knows I'm a bad mom, and he hates me for it," or "She's better off growing up without me because I can't do a good job."

These dysfunctional thoughts come from early life experiences that you've internalized. They influence how you think about yourself. Often, the critical inner voice comes from your parent or primary caregiver. So, don't be surprised it sounds like your mother is inside your head.

In some cases, the voices take on the form of interactions you have with siblings, peers, or people with authority.

To seize power from this dysfunctional thought process, you must first accept that motherhood doesn't give you room for perfection. You might wonder, "What does this mean?" You're about to find out.

ACCEPTING THAT THERE IS NO ROOM FOR PERFECTIONISM IN MOTHERHOOD

Anxiety is a natural response to protect your baby and often manifests as hyper-vigilance and hyper-awareness. That's why you probably always find your mind racing: *What if my baby slips underwater during a bath? What if she suffocates during sleep? What if someone breaks into my house and takes my baby away?*

Usually, this is just mental noise created and amplified by your critical inner voice. If you dismiss the thoughts, they will eventually stop coming up.

On the other hand, these worries can become irrational to the point where you have an intense fear that something will happen if you're not constantly with your newborn. They can get out of hand and interfere with your ability to function. Once anxiety begins to overshoot reality, it becomes a problem.

Every mother, including experienced ones, struggles with these fears and anxieties. Yet, we shy away from talking about it. There are many reasons why post-partum mothers don't share their scary thoughts and voices.

- **Ambiguity**

New moms don't talk about destructive thoughts in their heads because they don't know if it is normal or problem-atic. This is because new moms with postpartum depres-sion have overlapping experiences with new moms who have no such diagnosis.

For instance: weight changes, fatigue, moodiness, loss of libido, low energy, and sleep disturbance are common symptoms of anxiety and depression, yet they're also commonly experienced among women who adjust to postpartum life normally.

Since it's normal for women's internal experiences to fluctuate during the postpartum phase, new moms often decide they're better off braving all discomfort, hoping it will disappear in time.

Unfortunately, you can ride out dysfunctional thoughts. These scary thoughts can rapidly move from simple worries to intense panic if left unchecked.

- **Shame**

An intense feeling of shame often accompanies negative thoughts. *What is wrong with me? Why am I having such terrible thoughts? A good mother shouldn't be thinking these things.* Often, the only rational answer new mothers come up with is that there's something profoundly wrong – they believe something is broken within them. *Perhaps I'm not fit to be a mother. Or maybe I'm close to insanity.*

Of course, none of these options are good. So, that feeling of shame stuns women into silence. They silently hope that the scary thoughts will somehow go away with a bated breath. In some cases, the thought goes away. Usually, they remain.

Other mothers work tirelessly to eliminate the thoughts from their minds, but those thoughts always seem to come back in full force. While some can express the horror of their inner thoughts and the intense shame accompanying them to a confidant, many fear talking about them will make the thoughts come alive. So, they keep them locked inside.

Women who express their thoughts often feel ashamed, embarrassed, mortified, guilty, and humiliated. They are sickened and repulsed by their thoughts. Some believe only a monster could create those thoughts. A key point is the high distress negative thoughts trigger in new moms.

The critical inner mom voice typically fuels shame-based obstructions to disclosing dysfunctional thoughts. You may be reluctant to discuss them with others because you:

> Believe the thoughts indicate there's something wrong with you.
> Fear that you're the only mom with these thoughts, and no one else would understand.
> Fear that saying it out loud will make the thoughts become a reality.
> Believe that good mothers don't have these negative thoughts.
> Hate yourself for thinking these things.
> Feel an overwhelming sense of shame and guilt.
> May not be comfortable expressing yourself, in general.

• **Stigma**

Many mothers say they worry about being labeled or stigmatized. Although new moms often feel a sense of relief in knowing that most women have similar experiences, some continue to feel burdened by what people might think or say behind their backs.

The stigma attached to being a new mom creates an oxymoron: It only ends up impeding postpartum recovery by weighing heavily on the heart of a woman trying her best.

Common obstructions relating to what people might think are:

- Worry that others will judge and label you as a bad mother.
- Worry that your partner will deem you incapable of caring for the infant.
- Concerned about confidentiality and what may happen if you reveal your inner thoughts to others.

My point is that if you aren't careful, the inclination to condemn your thoughts and actions in any way pushes the authority of those thoughts in a different direction, which can empower them even more.

As someone just venturing into motherhood, you must understand that you cannot be too hard on yourself because of what the critical inner mom voice says inside your head. There are no perfect mothers. Every mother struggles with negative thinking, and it's especially harder for women who experience postpartum anxiety and depression.

Changing your situation will be harder if you don't seek an intervention right now. You may spend the rest of your life haunted by the thought that you aren't good enough or that something bad will happen. And you will have no inner peace.

MOTHERHOOD AND IMPOSTER SYNDROME

I learned what imposter syndrome was when I had my daughter. Until then, I had never really experienced it – although I was faintly familiar with the idea. After a few days at the hospital, it was time to head back home. I had spent much of my pregnancy reading books, taking courses, and seeking advice from mothers around me. Yet, I wasn't ready for the wave of imposter syndrome that hit me.

I started panicking internally as soon as we checked out of the hospital. I wondered why the doctors let me leave with the baby. A part of me thought, "Do they realize I don't know what I'm doing? They shouldn't have let me leave!"

I wished I could remain at the hospital for a few more days. After all, it couldn't hurt to spend extra hours with nurses who were qualified – unlike me – to care for babies. When we reached home, and I spent my first night away from trained nurses as a new mom, I concluded that I wasn't ready for this new role.

Soon, I found out that I wasn't alone in this feeling. And I want you to know that you aren't alone in this.

Motherhood, especially the first experience, is often full of doubt, so it's not surprising that many women struggle with a form of imposter syndrome.

If you don't know what imposter syndrome is, the term was introduced to the world in 1978 by two psychologists, Pauline Rose Clance and Suzane Imes. It is the internalized feeling that our success is due to luck rather than hard work.

Imposter syndrome often creates doubt in your talents, skills, or accomplishments – with a fear that you will be exposed as a fraud or failure at any point.

Many mothers experience this, so much so that experts created a term known as motherhood imposter syndrome. If you've ever doubted your parenting skills, know you aren't alone.

The thing about imposter syndrome is that it affects how you think about yourself and how you believe others perceive you. You may sometimes feel like other mothers around you have it more together than you do. This can make you feel like you're missing the passing mark on good parenting.

As a mother, the belief that you are a fraud who isn't good enough can be harmful, especially due to societal expectations that women must navigate motherhood seamlessly and without challenges. This condition is amplified by believing you've fallen short of these expectations.

Even when praised for your efforts, you may secretly believe you're only fooling yourself and the people around you. You may struggle with guilt or worry that you're harming your baby, sometimes resulting in burnout.

Signs of motherhood imposter syndrome include:

- Perfectionism
- Frequently comparing yourself to other mothers
- Negative self-talk
- Self-doubt and self-criticism
- Feeling like a failure
- Finding it hard to ask for help
- Isolating from people
- Not wanting to return to work after your maternity leave
- Worry that others are judging you
- Postpartum insomnia
- Fatigue and exhaustion

Imposter syndrome can negatively impact your everyday life and relationship with your partner, friends, and family. Struggling with a nagging and overwhelming feeling of inferiority can leave you debilitated if not addressed.

It's okay if you feel unprepared for motherhood. After all, you didn't get any prior training before you were thrown into it without a manual.

You must learn to take comfort in knowing you started this journey with a little idea of what to do. Sure, you may have helped raise your siblings or babysat during adolescence. Maybe you've had a journey as a nanny in the past. That doesn't mean you feel completely prepared for your life as a mother.

You will struggle with certain things, but at the same time, you will learn about motherhood at an impressive rate. Months or years later, you will reflect on these early days and laugh at yourself for being naive. You will also appreciate your growth.

The important thing right now is to be gentle with yourself. Take every day as an opportunity for learning and growth. Of course, to do this, you must learn to silence your inner critic – not just in parenting but in other areas of your life as well.

Start by reminding yourself now and then that you're the mother your child needs. While it's easy to look around you and believe other women excel at this much more than you, remember that you're the perfect mother for your newborn. Certain days may feel like a train wreck as you navigate this journey, and you will still be the mom your baby needs.

Here are some tips to help you overcome or minimize imposter syndrome.

- **Talk about it.** The mere idea of doing this can be awfully scary, but talking about how you feel can help reduce the hold imposter syndrome has over you. Vocalizing your struggle is an excellent way to acknowledge and normalize it. Speak freely about your mistakes and lessons. Accept that you're learning on the go and doing your best.
- **Know the difference between thought, feeling, and action.** Thinking or feeling inadequate at parenting doesn't mean you are. Train your mind to differentiate between what you think, how you feel, and what you do. A great way to do this is to acknowledge when you do something, such as decluttering a room. Reward yourself with an appreciative thought like, "I made my bedroom beautiful."
- **Set realistic goals.** Focus on things you can achieve daily, and have realistic expectations. Most importantly, celebrate your wins – no matter how small.

There are no easy paths to getting through motherhood. It is the hardest job you'll ever have to do. When you feel you're a fraud, remember that you aren't alone and are the perfect mom for your child.

HOW TO REFRAME YOUR NEGATIVE THOUGHTS

If you're wondering how to stop the never-ending buzz of criticism, nagging, slurs, and nitpicking in your head regarding your parenting skills, I have the perfect solution for you.

Cognitive reframing is your best tool for silencing your inner critic mom's voice. It involves learning to identify and reframe unhelpful thought patterns. Negative thoughts are automatic. Often, you don't even know when they pop into your head. And even when you know them, they seem perfectly reasonable to you. The thing about negative thoughts is they are super creepy. You might start thinking, "I don't know how to parent," out of nowhere.

Fortunately, you can tackle negative thoughts by reframing them. If it doesn't come naturally, you must train your brain to challenge and reframe negative thoughts.

How does cognitive reframing work?

- First, step back when you catch your inner critic at work and identify a negative thought.
- Next, evaluate the thought and challenge it with indisputable proof in the form of a fact.
- Finally, replace the negative thought with a positive one. This is crucial to the process.

For example, if "I look so fat after giving birth" pops into your head, acknowledge it's a negative thought. Then, challenge it: "I have been working out daily, and my partner even acknowledged my progress the other day." Finally, reframe the thought with, "I just gave birth, and I look good. I shouldn't be hard on myself. I will make my recovery if I keep putting in the work."

Below, I have three common negative thoughts among new moms and how you can reframe them.

- **"I'm bad at parenting."**

When you have your first child, it's normal to be over-whelmed by the enormity of your new responsibilities. Many new moms worry that they aren't 'natural' at parenting. They find parenting harder than they expected it to be.

The thing about being a new parent is that you have to learn on the job. Yes, some of it will come down to intuition. Still, you will get better with each day. As a new baby is born, so is a parent – don't expect to know everything as soon as the baby comes, just as you wouldn't expect your infant to start walking or crying the day they were born.

Reframe: "I am new to this and capable of learning and improving. There is no such thing as a perfect parent. Making mistakes is a part of the learning curve."

Anytime you think you're bad at parenting, reframe the thought immediately.

- **"I can't ask for help. It's a sign of weakness."**

Despite what many think, asking for help isn't a sign of weakness. I believe it to be a show of strength. Are you familiar with the saying, "It takes a village to raise a child?' Well, this saying was created because parents across different cultures throughout different generations understood that parenting was so challenging that the responsibilities had to be shared.

Reframe: "Asking for help isn't a sign of weakness. My family and friends have said I can come to them for anything I need."

Remind yourself that asking for help isn't a sign of weakness. That is why you build a support system, so don't be afraid to ask or accept help when it's offered.

- **"My baby doesn't like me."**

I have met many new moms who believed their babies didn't like them. They somehow thought the infant could sense their inadequacies. As a result, they feel like they can't form a bond with their kid.

If this happens to you, know that this belief is unfounded. It is impossible for a newborn not to like their primary caregiver. Don't be hard on yourself if you don't feel an instant bond with your child. In time, you will bond naturally with your child as you adjust to life together.

Reframe: "I love my baby, and he loves me. He smiled at me just now, so he definitely likes me a lot."

Spend quality time with your child and make skin-to-skin contact multiple times daily. This can help with bonding and make you feel closer to the infant.

Note: You won't become skilled at reframing in one day. It requires consistency and daily practice for success.

THE PROVEN BENEFITS OF POSITIVE AFFIRMATIONS

You are most likely familiar with positive affirmations, even if you've never tried them. I and nearly everyone in the 21st century have heard about the power of positive affirmations. But if you've never tried them, the idea can seem ridiculous. And when you do try them, you may feel just a little awkward. I did, too, the first time I practiced my daily affirmations.

Telling yourself you're an awesome mother can seem bizarre, but effective ways exist. And if you're a skeptic, that's fine. There is scientific evidence behind the power and popularity of positive affirmations, and we'll discuss them shortly. But first, let's define positive affirmations.

Positive affirmations are phrases or statements repeated to challenge unhelpful thoughts and rewire the brain to adopt positive thought patterns. Practicing positive affirmations is straightforward: simply choose a phrase and repeat it to yourself as many times as necessary.

You may use positive affirmations to motivate yourself, boost your self-esteem, or encourage positive growth. Suppose you frequently catch yourself engaging in negative self-talk. In that case, you can tackle those automatic, subconscious patterns with positive affirmations.

As mentioned earlier, the power and popularity of these short phrases and statements are based on well-established scientific theory.

Self-affirmation is a key psychological theory behind positive affirmations. It is based on the idea that we can maintain self-integrity by positively affirming our beliefs. Self-integrity relates to our "perceived ability to control moral outcomes and respond flexibly when our self-concept is threatened."

In short, human beings are motivated to protect themselves from perceived threats by maintaining self-integrity.

Numerous studies have shown that positive affirmations activate areas of the brain associated with self-processing and reward. It also helps to achieve neuroplasticity – the ability to rewire the brain.

The human brain cannot distinguish between reality and imagination, which is the loophole positive affirmations exploit. When you repeat a positive affirmation, your brain creates a mental image of that version of yourself in the affirmation. And when that happens, it activates the area of your brain that would be activated if that happens in reality.

But the more you repeat an affirmation, the more your brain is encouraged to accept it as a fact. And when it does, that, in turn, motivates you to take steps toward achieving that goal.

Here are some benefits of positive affirmations.

- Reduces negative thinking
- Reduces chronic stress
- Increases happiness
- Increases gratitude
- Reinforces positive thinking

Next, I have 20 affirmations you can practice daily. Choose any of these and repeat it to yourself aloud randomly throughout the day.

1. *I am a good mother.*
2. *I can take care of my baby.*
3. *I am the mother my baby needs.*
4. *I am good enough to be a parent.*
5. *My life is better than having this baby.*

6. *I welcome the challenges of motherhood with a warm heart filled with gratitude and love.*
7. *My feelings and experience are part of the great journey of motherhood.*
8. *I am loving and dedicated to my child.*
9. *I know my baby's needs, and I can meet them.*
10. *I was divinely chosen to be the mother of this baby.*
11. *I always make the best decision for my baby and me.*
12. *My bond with my baby grows stronger each day.*
13. *I adore my baby, and he adores me.*
14. *I open myself up to warmth and affection from my baby.*
15. *I am strong.*
16. *I am brave.*
17. *I am surrounded by people who love, respect, and support me.*
18. *I am open to accepting help from others.*
19. *I can and will endure anything that comes my way.*
20. *I am worthy of love and affection.*

When I was younger, my mom had a friend called Sarah. I remember when Sarah had just given birth. She was convinced her son hated her. According to Sarah, the baby always cried for no obvious reason. "Weird," I thought since the baby never cried when they came to my house. I concluded that the baby must hate her.

Knowing what I know now, that baby only picked up on Sarah's anxiety and tension. Of course, the baby didn't hate his mother. If only she knew how to reframe her thoughts, she would have learned to calm herself down, and the baby would have stopped feeling the tension.

New mothers struggling to find time for themselves probably find it hard to say "No" because of pleasing people. Unrealistic expectations and the need to be perfect can lead to saying yes when you want to say no. The next chapter explores how you can overcome this.

6

REASSESSING YOUR VALUES AND BELIEFS AS A MOM

> "Not forgetting who you are before the baby. You are still allowed to be you. Don't lose your identity. Add to it."
>
> — TIFFANY MARIE

We spend every minute of our life making decisions based on our beliefs and values. What we choose to invest time and energy into reflects our core values. Motherhood opens up an opportunity for you to sit with yourself and reassess your values. It creates such a change in your life that it becomes necessary to revise your goals to become your ideal self.

When I started to write this book, I had no intention of adding a chapter about values. But I remember musing for over a week on what I would include in the book that'll be helpful to new moms. Then, I briefly thought about how motherhood had me reevaluating my values, leading to me making life-changing decisions.

Before my first child, my core values were creativity, respect, recognition, knowledge, responsibility, and independence. Then fast forward to after having my third child, something changed within me. I became reflective and protective and felt needed by my kids. Suddenly, values like kindness and equality became more important to me.

I prioritized spending quality time with my kids and reflected on mindfulness meditation regularly. The more I met like-minded parents, the more I felt I had found my tribe and purpose.

After my maternity leave, I returned to work and felt out of place, not regarding work but values and emotions. I didn't know where I fit in the company anymore. Of course, I tried to realign, but it only got worse. Finally, I decided to talk to a mentor who was also a life coach.

My coach Carol laid the groundwork for reevaluating my beliefs and values. She said that I had to face my limiting beliefs. Three months of coaching made me realize my values were no longer the same. This wasn't anyone's fault, as motherhood had inevitably changed me.

A few months after coaching, my values looked like this: self-awareness, love, trustworthiness, respect, recognition, creativity, and integrity.

My renewed values pushed me to review my wants and needs in my personal and professional life. All of these culminated in me making major life-changing decisions. And now, I tweak my values every couple of years to stay attuned to my core values. I believe my life is aligned, and I truly feel like myself.

My point is, being a mother changes you. But that doesn't mean you must lose who you were before having a baby. Instead, you must reassess your core values, let go of those that don't align with the new you, and build on the existing ones that you cannot let go of.

But first, how do you determine your core values?

DO YOU KNOW YOUR CORE VALUES?

Have you ever sat down and tried to figure out the most meaningful things in your life? Usually, most people have vague ideas of the most important things and the things that make up their belief systems. It's important to take time to reflect on what matters to you and why so that you can truly understand what your core values are.

There is no better way to get to know yourself than by reflecting on the things that matter to you. While thousands of values exist worldwide, focusing on a handful of values that align with your innermost beliefs is much better.

It can be tricky to juggle multiple things simultaneously, and values are exempted. On average, most people have 5-10 core values they work hard to embody throughout their lifetime. Values are life's guidepost – they help you stay focused, prioritize what matters, and make decisions aligning with your beliefs and needs.

Reassessing your values after childbirth is important for the following reasons:

- **Understand yourself better.** Reviewing your values allows you to discover what resonates with you in motherhood and what doesn't. You may be surprised that there are still things you don't know about yourself. Yes, you've known yourself all your life, but that can make it hard to discover new things, especially if you don't self-reflect regularly. Exploring your values allows you to gain new insight into who you are now that you are a mother.
- **Influence decision-making.** It's hard to make decisions, especially if you consider social pressure. Knowing your values is akin to having a cheat code to bypass social pressure when making decisions. You can easily decide what aligns with your values and what doesn't and let that guide

your decision-making. This can boost your
confidence since no one has your back like you.

- **Set new goals and make plans.** Once you
reevaluate and understand your core values, you
can let that guide you in setting goals and making
plans. For example, if you value quality family
time, you could move from an urban area to a
closely-knit community. Understanding your
values is key to prioritizing and looking at the big
picture when making plans, setting goals, or
making decisions.

Values rarely stay the same, and they rarely change. Only
major life changes, like getting married, having kids, or
healing from trauma, can inspire you to reassess your
values. That's because you need time and life experience
to determine what deeply matters to you and what you
believe.

It's okay if you have different values at different stages of
your life. For example, you might value adventure as a
single woman, but that may shift when you become a
mother. Instead of seeking new adventures, you might
find that you'd rather be a homebody to spend as much
time as possible with your family.

There's nothing wrong if the things that matter to you
change with motherhood. Life wouldn't be as interesting
if everyone stayed the same for our whole lives. As you

navigate your life as a new mom, you will gain more insight into what works for you and what doesn't.

So, how do you find out what your core values are?

To an extent, your past experiences shape your values and how you incorporate them into your daily life. One effective technique that can help you reevaluate your value system is "Values Clarification." It comprises five simple steps and can be easily practiced in the comfort of your home.

Here's how to practice values clarification:

1. **Define yourself:** Introspect and try to determine what life means to you. Now that you're a mother, what are the qualities you have? Which qualities would you retain, and which would you let go of? Are there qualities that you want to develop, and why?

2. **Determine what drives you:** Think about different parts of your life, from motherhood to career to relationships. Explore the relationships you would like to attract going forward and why. Determine the qualities you want to exhibit at work. And finally, explore the kind of relationship you want with yourself.

3. **Identify what drives your emotions:** Write down a list of your triggers – i.e., situations that could elicit an emotional reaction from you, whether

positive or negative. Your emotional responses are most likely tied to core values you hold dear to heart. Once you identify your emotional triggers, you can explore that further to identify the associated values.

4. **Find out where you currently stand.** There's always room to improve and enhance your life. So, compare your values and beliefs to those you aspire to be. You may change your current perception attitude or lower the expectations for your ideal self to find common ground.

5. **Practice mindfulness.** Stay grounded in the present moment to maintain awareness of the values you exhibit daily. When you behave impulsively, take a moment to figure out the underlying reason for that behavior. Then, find a pattern and determine the potential values it represents.

HOW TO SET BOUNDARIES AND FOLLOW THROUGH WITH THEM

Few things reveal the necessity of having boundaries than becoming a mom. If you've ever tried to breastfeed in a room full of family after having your baby, you most likely know what I'm talking about.

Boundaries are guidelines you put in place to get people to respect your needs. They are necessary for all forms of relationships and different phases of life. But they are particularly important for new parents, especially moms with babies.

That is because boundaries are a critical part of self-care for new moms. They enable you to protect your physical and emotional needs, such as routines, sleep, privacy, downtime, schedules, and bonding moments with your infant.

Healthy boundary setting is key to maintaining meaningful relationships and connections. Because when you respect people's needs and vice versa, you're more inclined to give the best of yourself to them. So, don't feel like setting boundaries makes you selfish–it ultimately works for all parties involved.

Motherhood is such a huge change that when your baby arrives, your limits may change. As such, you may have to establish and enforce new boundaries. How you do that may look different from person to person and how you enforce them.

The fact is every mom is different, and that influences who we are in relationships. As a mother, you've likely received unsolicited advice on how best to parent – from friends, family, coworkers, neighbors, fellow moms, or strangers. It could even be from people whom you value their opinions.

So, figuring out how best to set and enforce boundaries with these people can be tricky. It can be even harder when doing this with your loved ones. Understandably, you don't want to hurt anyone's feelings. At the same time, not speaking up hurts your feelings. It can even hurt your relationship with these people in the long term.

With that in mind, here are six tips to help you set and enforce boundaries as you navigate parenting.

1. Consider what boundaries represent to you.

The purpose of boundary setting is to let people know what you'll tolerate and what you won't. Before you communicate that to others, you must begin with yourself. Reflect on what boundary setting means to you.

Did you grow up in a family that encouraged or discouraged having boundaries? Have you tried to set boundaries in the past? How did that make you feel – scared, nervous, or disrespectful? Or did you feel justified?

Consider what you think and how you feel about setting boundaries. Know that there are no right or wrong answers.

This first step makes you aware of how you perceive boundaries, as these perceptions will probably come up when you set or enforce them with others.

2. Identify your boundaries.

Now that you know what boundaries mean to you, continue to reflect and determine which areas you'd like to set boundaries in. Do you want to speak to your family about how you need to make the most of your time because you're busy with the baby? Do you want to discuss remarks from friends about how you feed your baby? Do you want to address comments about how best to care for your baby?

Write down everything that comes to mind. That will ensure you're clear about the boundaries you need to set.

3. Practice daily.

Role-playing can help you practice how best to communicate your boundaries with others. It can help boost your confidence as you prepare for potentially stressful conversations.

4. Prepare for all the worst-case scenarios.

I have observed that women recoil from setting boundaries with family because they're convinced it won't be received well or they won't be able to enforce them successfully. Combat this by preparing for all the worst-case scenarios your head can develop.

You'll find this particularly helpful if you can do the role-play with someone you trust. That can give you some much-needed assurance.

Still, whether or not you role-play with another person, remember that you aren't responsible for how others react to you setting boundaries. It may feel like that, but remind yourself the other person's behavior is their responsibility.

The more you practice, the better you will get at setting boundaries. You may be slightly anxious on your first few tries, but I promise you'll only get better.

LEARN TO SAY NO WITHOUT FEELING GUILTY

"Can you babysit my kids for a few hours?

"We would like you to volunteer at an upcoming school event. Do you mind?"

"Mom, I want you to make this recipe I found on Instagram."

So many requests from different people, and each time, you say 'yes' when you want to say 'no' deep inside you. This happens to moms, including me, all the time. We find it hard to turn people down – to say 'no' to things we don't want to do. No matter how exhausted, tired, burnt out, or depleted we are, there's that compulsion to say 'yes' when people make demands of us.

You're not alone in this, but the good news is there is hope for you yet. It took a long time for me to finally become used to saying 'no' instead of 'yes' to things I would rather not do. And I want you to get to this point, too – if you aren't already. I want to help you start saying 'no' and only say 'yes' when you mean it. As I like to say, 'no' to someone else is a 'yes' to your needs.

There are many reasons why moms feel like we must say 'yes' even when we need or want to say 'no.'

- **Socialization.** This is why women, particularly mothers, can't seem to say no. We're socialized to be likable and agreeable to fit into the social system.
- **Empathy.** Women tend to be more empathetic than men and more attuned to others' needs and feelings. This makes it harder to tolerate disappointing others. So, we find it easier to say yes.
- **Approval.** Sometimes, a woman's need to be of service stems from her upbringing and parenting. If you were raised by an authoritarian parent who punished you for disobedience or disagreement, you might need to behave agreeably to win their approval, even as an adult. Or if your parents were neglectful, you may have learned to "people-please" to get their acceptance.

- **Pressure.** Besides wanting to be liked, moms find it hard to say 'no' because we're socialized to show that we're strong and can do everything. This translates into wanting to care for the whole household as if we're the only resident and being there for our kids regardless of our needs or feelings. Doing anything less than that in your head indicates that you're failing at motherhood.

Now that you know why you're inclined to say 'yes' no matter how badly you want to say 'no,' let's examine the personal cost of always conceding to people's demands.

You might think saying 'yes' doesn't harm you in any way, but that's untrue. You inadvertently neglect your needs and feelings whenever you say 'yes' to something you don't want to do. And if this goes on for long enough, it often leads to disappointment, resentment, anger, anxiety, and depression. It might seem easy to avoid hurting people's feelings, but it only causes more harm than good.

Let's say your child asks you to make a recipe they got from their friend, and you don't want to because it would take a long time. But still, you say 'yes' to avoid a tantrum and keep the peace. You may not realize it, but that's how you teach your kids not to respect your boundaries or needs.

Learning to say "NO."

So far, we've established that saying 'yes' when you mean 'no' is a common mom problem. You want to make everyone happy and meet their needs. Yes, there is an underlying biological drive, but most stem from socialization. Now, the question is, how do you start saying 'no' when you mean no? Learning this can take a lifetime, but you can start from here.

- **Practice saying no.** You need time and practice to master when to say no. And the more you say it, the easier it becomes. So, practice saying 'no' and its many variations as often as possible.
- **Communicate clearly.** The clearer you are with your 'no,' the better the other person will respond. Clear communication is vital because it makes it harder for people to respect your boundaries if you are unsure. So, incorporate clarity and simplicity when saying 'no.'
- **Show gratitude.** If someone asks something of you, sometimes you must respond with more than a 'no.' Express gratitude to soften your delivery. It shows the other person you care about their feelings too.

In theory, most people understand why saying 'no' is important. But gathering the courage to implement it in real life can be scary and overwhelming. Therefore, you must have some guiding statements to help you.

Below are 10 statements you can use instead of 'no' when backed into a corner.

1. *"I have another commitment."*
2. *"I have something else going on."*
3. *"I wish I could, but I don't have the bandwidth for that right now."*
4. *"I'm honored to be asked, but it's not something I can do right now."*
5. *"I can't make time for this."*
6. *"I wish I could."*
7. *"Thanks for considering me. However, I'm unable to help."*
8. *"I'm sorry, but I can't fit this into my schedule."*
9. *"Unfortunately, I have plans. Perhaps another time!"*
10. *"That sounds lovely, but no, thank you."*

Assertive communication is a vital life skill. It allows you to express yourself effectively, stand up for your viewpoint, and protect your boundaries. More importantly, it allows you to do all this while respecting others' beliefs, rights, and feelings.

There are different communication styles:

- Assertive
- Passive
- Passive-aggressive
- Aggressive

If you're a passive communicator, you may go with whatever people decide for you to avoid conflict. But this sends a message that your feelings and needs aren't important, causing them to ignore your wants when making decisions or demands.

On the other hand, aggressive communication makes you come across as a bully who doesn't care about others' feelings and needs. It may make you seem self-righteous and morally superior. Being an aggressive communicator may get you what you want, but it leads to resentment.

The bottom line is that assertive communication is the best style. Your life experience informs your communication style. But here's how you can change to communicating assertively:

- Assess your current style to determine which changes you need to make.
- Use 'I' statements to communicate your thoughts or feelings without making people defensive. For instance, instead of saying, "You're wrong," say, "I disagree." Be clear, straightforward, and specific.

- Rehearse general scenarios and role-play with friends to practice assertiveness.
- Keep your emotions in check. If you're too emotional, wait for a while to collect yourself.
- Practice in low-risk situations, then gradually work your way up.

Learning to say 'no' when you mean 'no' takes time. It won't happen overnight, but keep pushing – you'll get there.

MOTHERHOOD SHOULD NOT BE YOUR GOAL

Women's goals always seem to change after having kids. Your success becomes less about your career and more about your parenting. But this doesn't have to happen. Women need to have goals that have nothing to do with being a mom. This can help us to maintain our own identity separate from being parents. You can aim to have a successful career and be a happy mom. No rule says you must forgo one for the other.

Here's a rundown of setting goals that align with your career, parenting, and personal growth.

- Write down your goals using the SMART framework – specific, measurable, attainable, relevant, and time-relevant.
- Create an action plan for each goal.

- Organize your time and space.
- Make time for your family in the plan.
- Step out of your comfort zone.
- Get people involved.
- Celebrate your milestones, no matter how small.
- Find extra help along the way.

I want to end this chapter by telling you about my friend, Tanya. Before childbirth, Tanya was career-driven and ambitious. But after she gave birth, she lost her identity, as many women do. Life became about her baby and that alone. There was no drive for everything else she wanted to achieve in life. That was until I advised Tanya to do a goal-oriented brain dump. This allowed her to realize that even though having a baby had changed her life forever, she still had existing and new goals she wanted to achieve. Fortunately, Tanya got her groove back.

Self-care means putting yourself first from time to time, and your partner may find this hard to understand. Self-care requires self-love; you shouldn't need others' love or validation to feel satisfied or complete.

At the same time, your relationship is a crucial part of your identity. And naturally, it'll need extra attention after you have a baby.

7

WHEN RELATIONSHIPS NEED TLC

> *"Your relationship with every single person will change."*

— NIKKI MARIE

Perhaps you never truly fought with your partner before the baby. Now it seems like there's always something to argue about every week. If this sounds familiar, you aren't alone – even if there are no fights and you feel differently toward your partner.

Motherhood changes your relationship with everyone, including your partner, friends, and family. It's a big transformation, so this isn't exactly surprising. After all, you're tired, sleep-deprived, and have no time to put other people first anymore – at least, that's what it looks like from your perspective.

Doing nothing will only make your relationships deteriorate, though. You may argue about the simplest things, from tasks to chores. So, it would be best if you were deliberate about making your relationship remain the same after a newborn and working harder to improve it.

This may sound like a lot of work, considering that you already have a lot on your hands. But you should know that it's normal for these changes to happen, and you only need to work through the issues with your partner.

Tiredness is one of the biggest reasons for tension and conflict after becoming parents. You have much less time to cater to other people's needs like you used to before the baby. There's barely time to hang out and enjoy what you used to before childbirth. As such, your partner feels left out. And if you don't feel like they're pulling their weight, you might resent them for that perceived lack of support.

Contrary to what society would have you believe, being a woman doesn't automatically make you a good listener or communicator – especially when hormones are in the mix. So, this chapter is all about helping you to see how childbirth may affect your partner and help you empathize with the changes they also go through.

More importantly, we will look at steps you can take to improve communication and strengthen or rekindle your relationship after having a baby.

Let's get to it.

COMMON RELATIONSHIP UPS AND DOWNS FOR NEW PARENTS

Many things, from tiredness to lack of sleep, can contribute to relationship ups and downs after having a child. And sometimes, couples' approach to dealing with issues such as lack of sleep contributes to the problems even more. New parents barely have time for other things. Time previously spent socializing, relaxing, or doing chores sharply reduces, changing the dynamics of our relationship.

Money – or a lack of it – can be a major stressor for new parents. Many have to adjust to life on one income, which can be challenging. This leads to money rows underpinned by emotional issues, such as the pressure of providing or the loss of financial independence.

As a mom, you may adjust to life at home with a baby instead of going to work. So, it helps to know the underlying issues that could fuel tension between you and your partner so that you can address that.

- **The transition from two to more.**

One of the leading factors for conflict is the transition from two to three or more. With a first baby, two people that used to be the most important person in each other's lives now have a more important person to put first. This transition can be hard for any parent that isn't the primary caregiver, as they struggle to accept they are no longer their spouse's top priority.

Your partner may feel sidelined as you focus on the child. Equally, you may feel invisible as everyone else fusses over the newborn. This could make you feel like your only role is to cater to the infant's and the entire family's needs rather than be a person in your own right.

You and your spouse must acknowledge how roles have changed and how you feel about that.

- **Different parenting styles.**

Some new moms find they have different parenting views from their partners, leading to conflict. As the primary caregiver, you may deem yourself the 'expert,' thus undermining your partner's confidence. Sometimes, new moms want their partner to do more but prevent them from doing so by micromanaging everything to do with parenting.

It's okay for your parenting style to conflict with your partner's. The key is to work together as a team and compromise on different issues.

- **Transactional communication.**

Since you and your spouse take turns sleeping, finding time to talk to each other might be hard. And when you do find time, your conversations may be primarily about the baby. In such a case, your discussions may come across as demands, leading to irritation on both sides. Caring for a newborn makes it harder to invest your time and energy into activities that strengthen a relationship.

- **Lack of spontaneity.**

Maybe you and your spouse used to go on spontaneous date nights before the baby. And now, there's simply no time for that. Spontaneity preserves the excitement in a relationship; with that gone, things can become pretty bland. Just preparing for an outing requires you to plan and prep and plan, making the outing seem like a chore rather than something to enjoy.

- **Physical intimacy.**

The intimacy aspect of a relationship can change drastically due to exhaustion, the demands, and the physical and emotional effects of childbirth. Everything works together to prevent you from wanting sex with your partner – no time, your body is all over the place, and there's resentment or irritation with your partner.

Plus, changing dirty diapers 12 times a day doesn't exactly put you in the mood. Also, some new moms experience vaginal dryness when breastfeeding. It may take time for you to feel like being intimate again after having a newborn.

Dealing with this requires a positive approach involving understanding your partner's needs, patience, and willingness to find new ways of displaying physical affection until you're ready to be intimate again.

Despite these tough hits that affect nearly all relationships after the arrival of a newborn, you can exploit this to make your bond with your partner stronger and deeper. Know that you're more than a pair now; you're a family.

Working through the rough stuff builds a powerful foundation for your family to survive the ups and downs of parenthood.

This isn't common knowledge, but men also experience hormonal changes after childbirth. You may find this surprising – I did when I found out. Awareness of possible hormonal issues your partner may be going through can help you determine how best to approach your relationship issues.

HANG ON – MY PARTNER HAS HORMONAL CHANGES?

New moms undergo many physical and emotional changes due to childbirth, but that doesn't mean men sail smoothly through the nine months and the months after.

Men's bodies and hormones change in many ways as they get accustomed to fatherhood.

- **Lower testosterone**

Testosterone is the number one manly hormone responsible for male aggression, sex drive, etc. Research suggests that women are more attracted to men with higher testosterone levels. Compared to thousands of years ago, this hormone has evolved to motivate men to find partners for procreation. When testosterone levels drop in men during or after pregnancy, they will likely be more involved in household chores and baby duties. In fact, the greater the drop, the more involved a dad is in parenting.

- **More oxytocin**

Oxytocin is the love hormone. Its production increases in women during pregnancy, labor, or breastfeeding, allowing moms to bond deeply with their newborns. In the past, science believed only new moms had higher oxytocin levels, flushing them with feel-good hormones to bond with their babies. Now, we know that new dads also get an oxytocin boost.

New research shows that new dads have higher oxytocin levels than non-dads. Interestingly, oxytocin production in moms is triggered when we comfort our kids. In contrast, it's triggered in men playing with their kids.

- **Brain changes**

Besides these major hormonal changes, new dads' brains also undergo some changes. Often, dads' brains mirror the same changes new moms go through. By three months postpartum, the parts of the brain associated with empathy, attachment, and nurturing expand and thicken up.

Of course, these hormonal changes new dads experience are minor compared to what new moms experience. But now you know you aren't the only one who hormonally changed due to parenthood.

EMPATHY FOR YOU, EMPATHY FOR HIM

Transitioning to fatherhood isn't just hard for women and men. Whenever I speak to new dads, they always mention how they imagined their biggest challenge would be stepping up their game.

They anticipated picking up more chores than usual or going through work in a sleep-deprived blur. And usually, they're resolved to make the meals, do the dishes, or do anything else a preoccupied mom can't get to herself.

Like typical men, new dads imagine problems they can solve by 'acting,' never thinking about the emotional aspect of fatherhood. The thrill of welcoming their newborn may not diminish for many expectant or new dads. Still, the infant's arrival can trigger a disorienting phase of powerful and turbulent emotions.

Just as new moms are predisposed to mood swings in the early days of parenting, new dads are at risk for anxiety and depression too. Unfortunately, society doesn't exactly empathize with new dads due to how we perceive emotional expression in men.

I once talked to a new dad who said he didn't expect fatherhood to be such an emotional roller coaster in the first few weeks. According to him, there was already significant pressure on him as the breadwinner. Then, you had the near shock of added responsibility as a father – the pressure of being responsible for two people and learning that his relations with his child can significantly influence the child's development. He felt understandably overwhelmed.

Another dad told me how hard it was to accept that he couldn't "fix" a fussy or crying baby as someone with a problem-solving mindset. He felt he had no control over anything and couldn't decide how best to react or respond to this unfamiliar issue.

The immediate period after childbirth can be exceptionally hard on men. Many new dads don't know whether other dads experienced similar emotional exhaustion and fatigue. So, they feel guilty having these feelings.

The key problem is that new moms are encouraged to verbalize their feelings about parenting, including disappointments, disillusions, and concerns. We are encouraged to do this to other moms or in support groups. In contrast, new dads cannot express their needs or feelings.

Even though they experience stress and anxiety about the newborn's arrival, fathers are expected to suppress their feelings. This isn't sustainable, leading to sleep problems, mood swings, and depression in many new dads.

For example, after childbirth, fathers sometimes need physical and emotional space. But they risk being criticized for taking alone time and can't verbalize their needs without appearing insensitive or uncaring. Such a cycle can throw a new dad into a depressive loop.

Another reason a new dad might refrain from sharing his struggle is the preoccupation of many new moms with their babies. Typically, daddies feel sidelined as the mommies' innate nurturing instinct takes over.

Your partner might feel like their feelings and needs no longer matter as they watch you become hyper-focused on the newborn's needs. Or he might feel like, "I shouldn't add to her stress. At least not right now." seeing how hard you're working with the baby.

No doubt, motherhood is one of the hardest times of your life. But crazy hormonal moments can have you assuming that there's a lack of enthusiasm, interest, or support from your partner when really, he is going through his own emotional ups and downs.

You must try hard to see things from your partner's point of view. This will help with communication and bonding.

COMMUNICATING YOUR STRUGGLES

Somewhere between the excitement fueled by their baby's arrival and the postpartum struggles, many new parents experience a breakdown in communication. This makes sense considering you have just undergone a massive life transition, and priorities are no longer the same. Add that to new cranky sleep-deprived days and more financial responsibilities, and you can see how it makes sense for communication to decline.

Luckily, you can take steps to ensure your communication doesn't fizzle. All you need to do is reinvent it, and your relationship will be stronger.

Communication is crucial in a relationship but arguably more crucial after the arrival of a newborn. It is necessary to build an understanding of your viewpoints as new parents. Talking to your partner daily – about how you feel and what you're doing – is a vital way to connect. It's also helpful for preventing or resolving conflict.

This means you must learn to communicate your struggles together in positive ways. What you say is just as important as how you say it. Your words and body language can influence how your spouse receives and responds to your messages.

Constructive communication is achievable with these simple steps.

- **Pick your moment.** Whenever you have something to discuss with your partner, do it when you're calm and have the time to listen – like when the baby is asleep. Suppose you have to wait until an issue has passed to discuss it. Sometimes, you must let little things go and focus on issues that truly mean something to you. Ensure an issue is important before bringing it up with your partner.
- **Show genuine interest.** If your partner tries to discuss something, you must show them that you're genuinely interested in what they have to say. Stop whatever you're doing, focus on them, maintain eye contact, pay attention, and express agreement with nods and facial expressions. Be present and engaged – don't let less important things distract you.
- **Be positive.** Everyone wants to feel appreciated, so acknowledge your partner's help with the baby and around the house. For example, "I appreciate you staying up to watch the baby." If you consistently praise and encourage your partner, they will likely listen when you raise issues.

Communication is much easier when you approach it positively.

- **Be understanding.** It helps to demonstrate empathy, compassion, and support to your partner.
- **Offer your support.** Always take your partner's side in an upsetting situation. Make it an "Us vs. the world" thing. Don't side with the opposition, no matter what.
- **Create solidarity.** Take time to reminisce about simpler times before the baby, laugh through your tiredness, or fret over your baby together. Find solidarity together in the highs and lows of parenthood.
- **Show similarities.** Express your emotional struggles to your partner. This shows them you are on the same team and can relate to their feelings.
- **Show affection.** Hug your partner, hold their hand, rub their shoulders, and find ways to comfort them when they talk about their day or anything.
- **Help each other to process.** Offer to assist them in finding solutions to their problem. But remember, you're there to offer support, not solve their problems for them.
- **Listen fully before offering solutions.** Wait for them to express their feelings and then ask if they'd like your suggestions.

Communicating shouldn't only happen when there's conflict. Set aside time to regularly share your thoughts and feelings while enjoying each other's company. Overall, this will be great for your relationship and communication. And it helps to practice for when there's a real problem.

HOW TO RELIGHT THE SPARK

Needless to say, as soon as self-care becomes a regular part of your routine, it becomes easier to see yourself as not just a mom but a woman. While it's important to settle well into your new life, parents, you must still find ways to bond with your partner after the baby's arrival.

Here are some tips on how you can bring the passion back post-childbirth.

- **Forget the parent roles.** It sometimes helps to forget the parental roles and obligations and spend time with each other as a couple to relight the spark in your relationship after a child. Bring a babysitter, friend, aunt, grandparent, or other trusted persons over to watch your baby for an hour, through the afternoon, or a full night. Take that time to revisit activities you used to love before becoming parents. The goal is to regularly remind you of why you became a couple – to remember what attracted you to each other in the first place.

- **Take things as slowly as necessary.** It's okay if you're scared of postpartum sex. After all, your body just went through a pretty traumatizing event. You may not be ready for intercourse, and that's fine. Still, it helps to find other ways of being intimate with each other. Engage in contact activities that aren't orgasm-focused.
- **Be creative.** Don't be afraid to think outside the box when spending time together or being physically intimate. You can handle any parenting curve life throws at you as long as there's a creative approach.
- **Take a break.** Delivering a newborn can have a woman feeling dry, sore, and not-lubricated. Know that this has nothing to do with your desire for your partner. It's your hormones at work again. Giving your body a break can help you navigate the process safely.
- **Cater to your physical and mental needs.** This plays a huge role in intimacy between new parents. Stay hydrated, spend time outdoors, and do other things that make you feel good.

Above all, be willing to show greater love than before you became a family. Don't force your relationship to return to its state before the baby. Instead, acclimate to the new changes and get creative with spending time together.

SELF-CARE THROUGH INTIMACY

Postpartum intimacy is about more than the physical act of intercourse. And having sex after a baby isn't just down to physical recovery. It depends on factors such as:

- Sexual drive and motivation
- General state of health
- Emotional readiness for sexual intimacy
- Adaptation to your new role as a mother
- Ability to preserve your identity as a sexual being
- Relationship with your partner

Every woman has a unique experience post-pregnancy. So, it's hard to define what's normal regarding readiness for sexual intimacy. You have to consider your emotional health and make the best decision.

Contrary to belief, there's no scientific timeline for abstinence after childbirth, but the generally recommended timeframe is 4-6 weeks after having the baby. Overall, though, it all depends on your comfort level and desire.

If you've fully recovered physically, it's still okay if you don't want to resume sexual intimacy yet. This could be due to hormonal changes, sleep deprivation, postpartum depression, decreased estrogen levels, body image issues, etc.

It's best to resume sex only when you're ready and comfortable. But in the meantime, here are other things you can do to increase intimacy:

- Self-pleasure
- Outercourse
- Intimate experiences
- Rituals
- Movement
- Into-me-i-see
- Get naked without sex
- Make small gestures
- 'Quickies'

My friend, Alicia, confided in me about her struggles with her partner after childbirth. Like many women, she assumed that her partner was unsupportive and unwilling to be involved in their baby's care. She stereotyped his behavior, and this caused resentment to build on her side. Of course, this created many issues. Every day was an opportunity to argue about something trivial. Alicia was frustrated, and so was her partner.

Eventually, they decided to see a counselor who could help them learn to communicate with each other better. Through counseling, Alicia's husband revealed (ashamedly, according to her) that he was scared of making mistakes with the baby as a new dad. Despite her assumptions, Alicia's partner was simply afraid, like many new dads are.

The counselor was able to help them address issues relating to his fears and anxieties about becoming a father, and things naturally improved!

The final chapter of this book focuses exclusively on self-care. We will look at self-care activities and practices you can make a regular part of your routine without spending too much time. You will find that each activity can meaningfully impact your quality of life.

8

5-MINUTE SELF-CARE ACTIVITIES FOR SUNRISE TO SUNSET

> "*I don't believe you'll ever be 'you' again. And that's okay! You realize you're stronger than you ever thought and that you are capable of doing amazing things. So, in my opinion, I'm a different, new 'me' - a stronger 'me.'*"
>
> — DANI TALERICO

Time is everything for new mothers. You probably worry you can't fit self-care into your fully packed schedule.

So, I have made a list of daily activities you can complete in five minutes. They are simple and easy to achieve. And as you get used to them, you can add a few minutes at a time or extend your practice time at a stretch – it's all up to you. With time, you should feel encouraged to stop at different points in your day to take 5 minutes for self-care activities.

MINDFULNESS AND MEDITATION

Mindfulness and meditation are distinct yet similar. Mindfulness is a form of meditation, but you can practice it on its merit without meditating. Both allow you to focus on the present moment rather than fixate on the past or worry about the future. They allow you to tune in with your body and its needs. They are also very effective for improving sleep, regulating emotions, and boosting overall well-being.

A 5-minute mindfulness exercise daily is a great way to practice self-care and increase your happiness and contentment in life. You can achieve a mindful state of mind through various exercises and activities that ground you in the present and increase awareness of your thoughts, feelings, and sensations at any moment without judgment or criticism.

Here are some mindfulness exercises you can practice anytime, anywhere, in just five minutes.

- **Mindful breathing**

Breathing is an excellent way to recall yourself to the present moment. Whether caught up in your thoughts, stressed, frustrated, or anxious, bringing attention to your breath can help you stay grounded in the present moment. Plus, mindful breathing activates a state of calm and awareness that reduces stress and anxiety.

This exercise is as simple as sitting comfortably on your bed, chair, or the floor, closing your eyes, and focusing on the ins and outs of your breath from your body.

Follow these steps to practice mindful breathing anywhere and anytime:

> ➤ Sit comfortably and close your eyes.
> ➤ Take a few deep breaths and focus on them as they move in and out of your body.
> ➤ If you start getting tense, count each inhalation and exhalation.
> ➤ When you reach ten breaths, focus on the sensations in your body.
> ➤ Notice the sensations in your stomach, muscles, and lungs.
> ➤ Repeat for five minutes.

- **Breathe and stretch**

Improve your mindful breathing exercise by adding body stretches. This exercise requires you to sit in a quiet place to stretch peacefully. You may do it on your couch, chair, or anywhere else.

➤ Place your hands on your knees and assume a cross-legged sitting position.

➤ Push your chest forward and breathe in deeply.

➤ Arch your back and look up.

➤ Start breathing in slowly in this position with your spine curved up.

➤ Stretch your body in this way for at least 5 minutes.

- **Quick Yoga**

Yoga is one of the best ways to practice mindfulness. Different forms of yoga exist, but the common theme is slow, mindful movements. They can all help you practice breathing, poses, and meditation. Even if you are a Yoga newbie, you can try simple poses. Ensure you focus on making the pose rather than the end product.

This mindful yoga pose can loosen and stretch your hip flexors.

➤ Get on your hands and knees – on a mat, bed, or the floor.

➤ Place your right foot toward your right hand's outer part.

➤ Keep your right knee bent over your right ankle.

➤ Put your right hand inside your right foot.

➤ Focus on the stretch in your left hip.

➤ Slowly breathe in and out 5 times.

➤ Now, repeat with your left side and do 5 reps.

- **Body scan**

This is an exercise to put you in touch with your body. Sometimes, we don't notice changes happening within our bodies. A 5-minute body scan can help attune you to your body from the inside out.

➤ Lay down on your back comfortably with your palms facing up.

➤ Start a mental scan of your body from head to toe.

➤ You can start from the head and work down to the feet, or vice versa. Focus on one body part at a time.

➤ Notice how each body part feels. Do you feel tense? Sore? Is there discomfort in any part?

➤ After scanning your whole body, take some minutes to introspect.

➤ Write down anything that comes up in your journal.

- **Listen to the silence.**

Immersing yourself in the sounds of silence is a great way to practice mindfulness. We easily get caught up in the noise of everyday life and the chaos of parenting. It would help if you took five minutes out of your day to practice listening to the silence. It can help you keep in touch with yourself.

Try this exercise whenever you're in a quiet place with no distractions or waiting for something. You can also try it while commuting. Ensure your baby is asleep when you do this.

> ➤ Turn off all gadgets and devices.
> ➤ Put your pet outside.
> ➤ Sit in a quiet part of your home for five minutes.
> ➤ Soak yourself in the silence as you sit alone with your thoughts – or don't think at all.
> ➤ If needed, focus on a visual point.
> ➤ Stretch your body after 5 minutes and go about your day.

- **Mindful eating**

Savoring your food as you eat is a good way to ground yourself in the present moment. It will give you a whole new level of experience with your meals. So, whenever you eat, engage in the activity with all your senses – not just your taste. Be aware of the smell, its texture in your hand, the color of the food, etc. Savor the flavor and think about how it makes you feel.

- **Mindful coloring**

Regardless of your age, coloring is always a good way to focus your mind and practice being mindful. Get an adult coloring book and focus on painting whatever you want. It'll let you let go of overthinking or stress to focus on the moment.

- **Morning Coffee**

Take advantage of coffee's stimulating nature to ground yourself in the present. Focus on the taste, aroma, and sensation of coffee moving from your hand to your mouth down your throat. You'll be surprised at the rush of awareness doing this will give you.

- **Mindful gardening**

Gardening puts you in the center of nature, allowing you to interact and find a deeper sense of purpose. From watering to fertilizing your plants, ensure you engage all five senses when you garden.

- **Mindful showers**

Focus on the feel of water on your skin when you shower. Notice how it cleanses your body and pay attention to the immediate sense of cleanliness that washes over you.

- **Mindful chores**

Be focused on your chores at any particular time. Let go of distractions and engage your senses until you're done. You can support your daily mindfulness practice with guided meditation scripts. There are so many of them on YouTube.

DAILY JOURNALING

Writing down your thoughts and feelings throughout the day is another self-care activity I recommend to every new mom I meet. Being a mom can be incredibly rewarding and draining. Sometimes, you will feel overwhelmed. And in those times, journaling can help you gain clarity and refocus your mind.

However, knowing where to start processing your thoughts and feelings is hard. That's why I have a list of 20 journaling prompts that should be a part of your daily practice. Before you start, think about what you need at this moment to make journaling a part of your daily self-care routine.

While sitting down to write and introspect can feel tasking, it's a gift to yourself. So, set an intention and get appropriate supplies to make your journaling exercise meaningful and beneficial.

Here are the 20 prompts to help you clear your mind and process your thoughts and feelings.

1. *What is rewarding about my life right now?*
2. *What is hard about my life right now?*
3. *When was the most recent time I felt accomplished or appreciated?*
4. *How did that experience make me feel?*
5. *What is something I wish I could be celebrating at this moment?*
6. *What do I wish my parents had known when I was a kid?*
7. *What do I wish I knew about my parents?*
8. *What is something I wish was different about my life right now?*
9. *If I could go back in time before becoming a mom, what do I wish I realized?*
10. *What do I think about when I look at other moms?*
11. *What does my self-care routine look like? How can I improve it?*
12. *What routines or habits would make my life easier?*
13. *How am I similar to my mom? How am I different?*
14. *What am I grateful for in my spouse?*
15. *What is the number one thing I wish to teach my child?*
16. *How do I uniquely meet my kids' needs that no one else can?*
17. *How often do I feel isolated or lonely?*
18. *What mom do I look up to or respect? Why?*

19. *How has becoming a parent changed my views of my parents?*

20. *In what ways has motherhood changed me?*

You only need to spend 5 minutes journaling daily, so choose one question at a time. And let these prompts inspire you to develop newer prompts as you keep practicing.

DEEP BREATHING EXERCISES

Try any of these three deep breathing exercises to find stillness and calm whenever you feel too stressed or tired. Each can be practiced for only 5 minutes of your time every day.

Slow-Deep Breathing

> Inhale through your nose as you count to six to fill your lungs.

> Exhale through your nose as you count to six to empty your lungs.

> Count:"inhale-two-three-four-five-six; exhale-two-three-four-five-six".

> Count in your head until you fall into the breathing rhythm.

Square Breathing

> ➤ Inhale through your nose as you count to four.
> ➤ Hold your breath with your lungs full of air for a count of four.
> ➤ Exhale through your nose as you count to four.
> ➤ Hold your breath with empty lungs for another count of four.
> ➤ Count like inhale-two-three-four; exhale-two-three-four.

Counting Backward

> ➤ Place your hand on your belly and close your eyes.
> ➤ Breathe deeply through your nose and notice the rise of your belly under your palm.
> ➤ Breathe out through your nose and notice the fall of your belly.
> ➤ Count from 27 to 1 in your head as you inhale and exhale – 27 belly rises, 27 belly falls.
> ➤ Repeat for as long as 5 minutes allows you.

You can try these breathing exercises in a comfortable chair or on your bed to help you fall asleep.

5-MINUTE WORKOUT TO ENJOY WITH BABY

Being a new mom means you're busy 24/7 with your child, so you need to squeeze 5 minutes of workout into your schedule no matter how busy. To make this easier, I have created a list of 5-minute, energizing exercises you can try at home anytime, anywhere. These exercises not only work your whole body, but they also require minimal effort.

The sweetest thing about these moves is that you can do them with your baby front and center the whole time. You may find them an excellent avenue to bond with your child while getting your body back in shape.

Depending on your needs and preferences, you can try the routines separately or together every two days. Get your doctor's approval, and you can start working out as early as six weeks after childbirth. It may take longer if you had a Cesarean section for the birth.

Before you start the workout routine, here are some helpful tips:

- **Safety:** When doing the exercises where your baby must hold their head up, ensure the baby is at least 3-4 months old and can do so independently without discomfort. Otherwise, don't include those exercises in your workout routine.

- **Prep:** Roll your shoulders back and down to get your body ready, and pull your navel toward your spine for protection. Breathe through your nose to expand your ribs, then through your mouth to draw in your abdominal muscles.

Now, here are those exercises.

1. Dancing

Dancing is a simple exercise to get some cardiovascular workout involving your major muscle groups. It can improve balance and coordination and even boost your mood despite how stressed or tired you may be.

You can dance with your baby while holding them or put them in a strapped carrier to keep them close to your body. Put on good dancing music and dance away – be sure to draw your abs in throughout.

I recommend trying a variety of slow and fast music to elevate your heart rate but be careful with the baby as you bounce around. Take deep breaths or sing along to the music to monitor how exerting the physical activity is, and don't lose your breath.

2. Curl-Ups

Curls are excellent for strengthening your core muscles to improve lower back support. Lie on the floor with your face up, knees bent, and feet flat on the ground. Gently put your infant on or above your pubic bone. Secure the baby under their arms by wrapping your fingers around their torso.

Draw in your abs and slowly lift your head, neck, and shoulder from the floor on a count of two; lower on a count of three. Exhale deeply through your mouth as you lift, contracting your abs up and in. Repeat 15 to 20 times, rest for some minutes, then do another 15-20 reps.

3. Reverse Curls

Lie on the floor with your face up; bend your knees toward your chest; put your baby on your shins. Draw in your abs to tilt your hips up and lift your head, neck, and shoulder simultaneously. Then, lower and repeat 15-20 times. Rest a while and do another set.

4. Overhead Press

Overhead presses strengthen your back, shoulders, bicep, and triceps. Assume a cross-legged sitting posture to do an overhead press; hold your infant in front of your chest and bend your elbows. Now, stretch your arms upward, but don't lock your elbows. Pause, then gently lower your kid to the starting posture. Repeat ten times, rest, and then do two more sets.

5. Bench Press

Get on the floor, lie face up, and bend your knees. Draw in your abs and tightly squeeze your shoulder blades. Keep your baby close to your chest to secure them. Pause, then lower the baby to your starting position. Repeat 10 times, rest, and do two more 10 reps.

6. Plies

Do plies to tone your calves, buttocks, hamstrings, and quadriceps. Start by strapping your baby to their front carrier, ensuring their head is well supported. Start with two minutes of dancing to warm up, then do a minute of plies and one minute of walking lunges.

Alternate between these combinations for four minutes. Then, use the last minute to walk and cool down.

Stand with feet hip-wide apart to do the plies, turning your feet out a little. Contract your abs and bend your knees. Lower your hips and press your weight into your heels. Then, slowly stretch your legs and squeeze your buttocks as you return to standing.

7. Walking Lunges

Lunges do the same thing as plies. To practice lunges, stand upright and look straight ahead. Now, move your right leg forward and bend both knees until your front

174 | OLIVIA ROSE

knee is over your ankle and the back knee moves toward the heel. Finally, push off your back leg and move your feet together. Repeat with the second leg and keep going for 5 minutes.

I recommend trying 2-3 of these exercises daily and alternating as much as possible to ensure you don't repeat workouts on the same day.

TICKLE YOUR SENSES

This is a step exercise that can be very helpful in managing anxiety. It grounds you in the present when you find your head swimming in thoughts. Before you begin, focus on breathing – make it slow, deep, and long. This will help you achieve a sense of calm or calm you to a calmer mental state. Once your breath falls into a rhythm, follow these steps:

- Notice five things you see in your environment. It could be a spot on the wall, your shoe rack, the kitchen fridge, or anything.
- Notice four things you can touch in your environment: your pillow, the ground beneath your feet, or your skin.
- Notice three sounds you can hear. It could be your stomach grumbling or birds chirping outside your window. Acknowledge internal and external sounds.

- Notice two things you can smell. Perhaps the scent of your perfume or deodorant or your pillow. If necessary, walk to your bathroom to find the scent of your bathing soap, or go to nature outside and find the scent of wet grass.
- Notice one thing you can taste. Does the inside of your mouth taste like coffee, tea, or breakfast?

The 5-4-3-2-1 technique is great for when you feel overwhelmed by mommy duties.

LET IT OUT WITH MUSIC

Listening to music can be a self-care exercise for you to indulge in daily. I know it's my favorite part of my daily self-care routine. It stimulates good-feel thoughts, memories, and emotions. It also calms your nerves. Now, I don't mean just any type of music. I'm referring to calming music that can relax your nerves in five minutes.

During moments of stress, the right kind of music can bring you solace. It can distract you from worries or motivate you to move your body. Listening to music at home may not necessarily be music therapy. Still, you can use music to your advantage in many ways.

Here are tips:

- Start with music that matches your current mood, then gradually switch to music that matches your desired mood. For example, if you're feeling depressed, you can't start with happy music because you may find it off-putting or jarring. At the same time, you can't listen to sad music only because it will only make your mood worse. Therefore, it's better to match the music to your sad state to acknowledge your emotion. Then, after a while, change to groovy or upbeat music to get you to the emotional state you want.
- Move your body to the music to match the beat and rhythm of whatever you're listening to. When working out, play the music that matches your pace.
- Put on music that's relaxing to you whenever you want to calm down and achieve inner peace. As you listen, focus on your breathing and be aware of its movement in and out of your body.

Finally, use music to connect with the people you like. For example, you and your partner can make a collaborative playlist to listen to whenever you have your "us" time.

FIND LAUGHTER IN THE LITTLE THINGS

Laughter denotes joy, happiness, or celebration. It has plenty of physical and mental health benefits, including:

- Makes you gulp in large amounts of air, thus oxygenating your blood.
- Decreases the presence of stress hormones like cortisol and adrenaline to make you feel relaxed instantly.
- Strengthens your immune system.
- When you laugh, your body releases hormones and chemicals that can positively impact your system, such as endorphins – the feel-good hormone.
- A minute of laughter burns the same calories as spending 6-10 minutes running.
- Laughter boosts your mood. The fastest way to create a positive mental state is to laugh regularly as hard as you can.

Here are tips to help you laugh more.

- Resolve to laugh more; to find humor in your life as a new mom.
- Add laughter to your morning routine. You may set a reminder, reflect on something funny, and laugh deeply from your belly.

- Smile more to your baby, partner, friends, family, and strangers. Offer everyone a warm smile.
- Read funny stories or watch funny movies regularly.
- Make a funny friend.
- Watch your favorite comedian.
- Watch a funny sitcom like Friends or The Big Bang Theory.
- Get a dog – they're unbelievably funny.

To make incorporating these activities into your routine easier and make yourself more likely to practice daily, make a weekly calendar and add all seven activities into different parts of your day from Monday to Sunday. Do it according to your schedule. Once you finish an activity, check it off your calendar for the day.

Ensure you follow your self-care to-do list religiously.

CONCLUSION

Hey mama, I am so proud of you; well done for reaching the end!

I commend you for doing an incredible job reading this book from the beginning to the end. I hope it's been an amazing experience for you as it has been for me! But before I leave you to start executing all you've learned, I have a few words for you.

So far, you've learned the importance of loving your post-birth body. Despite the several changes your body will undergo due to hormonal shifts, you need to practice self-care and see the changes as reminders of the remarkable feat you've pulled off.

You learned the core values of self-care and how to implement them. We also highlighted the different practices to bring calm to your home.

You will experience a range of emotions in the first few weeks or months after childbirth. When skilled at recognizing your feelings and why they are there, it's easier to handle them, and to help you acquire these skills.

Reassessing your core beliefs, values and calming your inner voice negatively influencing you are crucial. You learned how to reframe negative thoughts, use positive affirmations, set boundaries, and how to prioritize yourself by saying *No* when it isn't convenient.

The last part of the book focused on Tender Loving Care and how to experience it in your home. You learned how to engage in different self-care activities that can be done in under 5 minutes.

I understand that you might struggle with your little one, and things may not turn out as you imagined. You don't need to beat yourself up because of that – it's all part of the parenting experience. So, regardless of your journey, you can use this book as your guide.

When I discovered the essential elements of self-care, I saw them as basic and wasn't sure they could give the results I wanted. Surprisingly, when I started paying more attention to my diet and taking short naps whenever my baby was asleep, I started noticing a significant difference in how I felt. I even made it compulsory to go to bed early and asked for help from my partner and anyone around whenever I needed it. I added many fruits and vegetables to my diet, drank more water, and reduced sugar and caffeine. I was hydrated and felt more alert.

However, I discovered a game-changer when I started taking time for myself. I started doing the things I enjoyed daily, even for just 5 minutes. It could be as simple as journaling, meditating, taking a walk, listening to my favorite songs, and even just enjoying a cup of tea.

Thanks to these elements I incorporated into my life, I focused more, felt energized, and enjoyed my new role as a mom.

Self-care is nothing to feel guilty about or something that is selfish. It doesn't take any attention away from your baby or your responsibilities. Instead, it empowers you and gives you the necessary mental and physical energy to get through the day, maintain a healthy relationship, and live the life you deserve.

Though, I am not perfect and still make mistakes. However, self-care doesn't mean I will always get it all right. I have the mental resilience to turn these mistakes into learning opportunities for myself and my family.

You don't need to feel overwhelmed trying to start every aspect of self-care all at once on top of the many other activities on your to-do list. If you don't feel like doing anything then close the book, put your baby to sleep, get comfortable, and just breathe. Then make a plan! You'll find the time for it.

SHARE YOUR HONEST OPINION

Finally, reviews are essential for authors, but you're doing something more significant when you share your opinion. Considering the prevalence of struggling new moms, your opinion on how self-care can show new moms that there is help available and that they can enjoy their motherhood experience. So if you've gained valuable knowledge and enjoyed reading this book, **kindly share your experience by leaving a review.**

Practice, practice, and practice all you've learned so far. As we end this journey, your new watchword should be *Read*, *Internalize*, and *Execute*.

Best wishes!

REFERENCES

American Psychological Association. (n.d.). Emotion regulation. Psychology Tools. https://www.psychologytools.com/

Baby Chick. (n.d.). How to Set Boundaries With Family When You Have a Baby. Retrieved from https://www.baby-chick.com/how-to-set-boundaries-with-family-when-you-have-a-baby/

Baby Chick. (n.d.). Why Moms Need to Learn to Say No. Retrieved from https://www.baby-chick.com/why-moms-need-to-learn-to-say-no/

Berkeley Wellbeing. (n.d.). Emotion Regulation. Retrieved from https://www.berkeleywellbeing.com/emotion-regulation.html

BetterUp. (n.d.). Emotional Regulation Skills. Retrieved from https://www.betterup.com/blog/emotional-regulation-skills

Bonomi, A. E. (2020). How to love your post-baby body. The Bump. https://www.thebump.com/a/how-to-love-your-postbaby-body

Cleveland Clinic. (2022). Postpartum weight loss: 10 ways to lose the baby weight. National Academy of Sports Medicine (NASM). https://blog.nasm.org/postpartum-weight-loss

CNET. (n.d.). 6 Ways Exhausted Moms Can Get More Sleep With a Newborn at Home. Retrieved from https://www.cnet.com/health/sleep/6-ways-exhausted-moms-can-get-more-sleep-with-a-newborn-at-home/

Colorado Springs Mom Collective. (n.d.). Emotional Intelligence Benefit Mothers. Retrieved from https://coloradosprings.momcollective.com/adversity/emotional-intelligence-benefit-mothers/

Daring to Live Fully. (n.d.). How to Laugh More. Retrieved from https://daringtolivefully.com/how-to-laugh-more

Dittmann, M. (2012). The grateful brain. Psychology Today. https://www.psychologytoday.com/intl/blog/prefrontal-nudity/201211/the-grateful-brain?eml

Ec.europa.eu. (n.d.). New fathers may undergo hormonal, neural, and behavioural changes. Retrieved from https://ec.europa.eu/

research-and-innovation/en/horizon-magazine/new-fathers-may-undergo-hormonal-neural-and-behavioural-changes

Everymom, T. (n.d.). Young Adult Fiction Novels. Retrieved from https://theeverymom.com/young-adult-fiction-novels/

Flora, C. (2018). The benefits of decluttering and self-care: Letting go can help you feel in control. The Simplicity Habit. https://www.thesimplicityhabit.com/decluttering-and-self-care-the-benefits-of-letting-go/

Gottman Institute. (n.d.). One Conversation New Parents Need to Stay Connected. Retrieved from https://www.gottman.com/blog/one-conversation-new-parents-need-stay-connected/

Happier Human. (n.d.). 5-Minute Mindfulness Activities. Retrieved from https://www.happierhuman.com/5-minute-mindfulness-activities/

Happier Human. (n.d.). Mindfulness Activities for Adults. Retrieved from https://www.happierhuman.com/mindfulness-activities-adults/

Hello Postpartum. (n.d.). Postpartum Hormone Timeline. Retrieved from https://hellopostpartum.com/postpartum-hormone-timeline/

Hello Postpartum. (n.d.). Family Boundaries & the New Baby. Retrieved from https://hellopostpartum.com/familyboundaries-new-baby/

Hinge Health. (n.d.). Filling Your Cup: The Importance of Self-Care. Retrieved from https://www.hingehealth.com/resources/articles/filling-your-cup-the-importance-of-self-care/

Holistic Parenting. (n.d.). How to Love Your Post-Baby Body. Retrieved from https://www.thebump.com/a/how-to-love-your-postbaby-body

Housman Institute. (n.d.). EI from birth to 5: Emotional intelligence benefits. Housman Institute. https://housmaninstitute.com/blog/ei-birth-5mental-health-benefits

Kindness Matters Guide. (n.d.). Retrieved from https://www.mentalhealth.org.uk/explore-mental-health/kindness/kindness-matters-guide

Kumar, R. (2022). How to stop comparing yourself to other moms.

Scary Mommy. https://www.scarymommy.com/parenting/how-stop-comparing-yourself-other-moms

Lola Lykke. (n.d.). Expert answers: How long does it take to fully recover after pregnancy? Lola Lykke. https://lolalykke.com/blogs/mamahood-manuals/expert-answers-how-long-does-it-take-to-fully-recover-after-pregnancy

Luciani, J. (2013). Emotional regulation: How to manage your emotions like a pro. The Everygirl. https://theeverygirl.com/emotional-regulation-how-to-manage-your-emotions-like-a-pro/

Marie, C. (2021). How to reframe your negative thoughts and break free from cognitive distortion. Marie Claire UK. https://www.marieclaire.co.uk/life/health-fitness/reframing-negative-thoughts-771750

Mom365. (n.d.). Items You Don't Have to Buy for Your Baby. Retrieved from https://www.mom365.com/baby/baby-gear/items-you-dont-have-to-buy-for-your-baby

Mom365. (n.d.). 10 Ways for Moms to Stick to Goals. Retrieved from https://www.mom365.com/mom/health-and-fitness/10-ways-for-moms-to-stick-to-goals

Mom.com. (n.d.). 5 self-care tips from celebrity moms like Michelle Obama. https://mom.com/entertainment/celebrity-moms-self-care-tips/michelle-obama3

National Sleep Foundation. (2022). The connection between diet, exercise, and sleep. Sleep Foundation. https://www.sleepfoundation.org/physical-health/diet-exercise-sleep

NASM. (n.d.). Postpartum Weight Loss. Retrieved from https://blog.nasm.org/postpartum-weight-loss

Peters, A. (2019). How I used a social media cleanse to get rid of postnatal anxiety. BabyGaga. https://www.babygaga.com/social-media-cleanse-got-rid-of-my-postnatal-anxiety/

Psych Central. (n.d.). Emotional regulation skills. Psych Central. https://psychcentral.com/health/emotional-regulation#skills

Psychology Today. (n.d.). The Grateful Brain. Retrieved from https://www.psychologytoday.com/intl/blog/prefrontal-nudity/201211/the-grateful-brain?eml

Psychology Today. (n.d.). How to Stop Comparing Yourself to Other

Moms. Retrieved from https://www.scarymommy.com/parenting/how-stop-comparing-yourself-other-moms

Psychology Today. (n.d.). Emotional Regulation. Retrieved from https://psychcentral.com/health/emotional-regulation#skills

Psychology Today. (n.d.). The Proven Benefits of Positive Affirmations. Retrieved from https://malpaper.com/blogs/news/is-there-science-behind-positive-daily-affirmations

SleepStation. (n.d.). Is rest as good as sleep? SleepStation. https://www.sleepstation.org.uk/articles/sleep-science/is-rest-as-good-as-sleep/

The Bump. (n.d.). 6 exercises for new moms. https://www.thebump.com/a/postpartum-exercise

The Bump. (n.d.). How to Love Your Post-Baby Body. Retrieved from https://www.thebump.com/a/how-to-love-your-postbaby-body

Thrive Leadership. (2018). Boost emotional intelligence by identifying triggers. https://thriveleadership.com/blog/2018/7/18/boost-emotional-intelligence-by-identifying-triggers

Therapist Aid. (n.d.). Gratitude Jar Worksheet. Retrieved from https://www.therapistaid.com/worksheets/gratitude-jar

Thrive Leadership. (n.d.). Boost Emotional Intelligence by Identifying Triggers. Retrieved from https://thriveleadership.com/blog/2018/7/18/boost-emotional-intelligence-by-identifying-triggers

UCL Institute of Education. (n.d.). Emotional Intelligence from Birth to 5: Mental Health Benefits. Retrieved from https://www.housmaninstitute.com/blog/ei-birth-5mental-health-benefits

UCSF Health. (2022). Nutrition guide for new moms. UCSF Health. https://www.ucsfhealth.org/education/nutrition-guide-for-new-moms

Upmc. (2019). Newborn support system. UPMC. https://share.upmc.com/2019/11/newborn-support-system/

Verywell Family. (n.d.). Self-care for new moms: A comprehensive guide. Verywell Family. https://www.verywellfamily.com/self-care-for-new-moms-4783220

West Music. (n.d.). Using Music for Self-Care. Retrieved from https://content.westmusic.com/using-music-for-self-care/

WebMD. (n.d.). Nutrition Guide for New Moms. Retrieved from

https://www.webmd.com/parenting/baby/nutrition-guide-new-moms

WebMD. (n.d.). New Dads: What to Expect. Retrieved from https://www.webmd.com/parenting/baby/features/new-dads-what-to-expect

WebMD. (n.d.). 6 Exercises for New Moms. Retrieved from https://www.webmd.com/parenting/baby/6-exercises-for-new-moms

WebMD. (n.d.). 6 Ways Exhausted Moms Can Get More Sleep With a Newborn at Home. Retrieved from https://www.cnet.com/health/sleep/6-ways-exhausted-moms-can-get-more-sleep-with-a-newborn-at-home/

WebMD. (n.d.). Is there a sex life after birth? 10 ways to bring back that lovin' feeling. WebMD. https://www.parentmap.com/article/is-there-a-sex-life-after-birth-10-ways-to-bring-back-that-lovin-feeling

YouMatter. (n.d.). Filling Your Cup: The Importance of Self-Care. Retrieved from https://youmatter.suicidepreventionlifeline.org/filling-your-cup-the-importance-of-self-care/

Zimmerman, M. A. (n.d.). Gratitude jar. Therapist Aid. https://www.therapistaid.com/worksheets/gratitude-jar

Made in the USA
Las Vegas, NV
13 November 2023

80782141R00105